Beyond Identities in Modernity

This book argues that future generations of modernity as a whole will shape participatory modernization whether Chinese modernization or Western modernization. The public discourse is inundated with the good and the bad modern events with the acceleration of globalization.

This book debates that the biggest question in the twenty-first century is not who will dominate, touting a new world order upon us, but rather that it is the orientation of modernization that haunts our daily realities. This book explores the idea that life is not about living for an identity in any society, it is about the demands for dignity and safety. It goes further to state that there is also a demand for the power of being, and these three elements are beyond identities as modernization moves forward. Interdisciplinary in nature, the book uses theories, data, and philosophy as toolboxes to align with micro realities around the globe. Witnessing modernization and modernizing identities in China and in Australia beyond day by day, the author provides a more suitable, more realistic, and possibly, more nuanced perspective.

This book will be of interest to professionals, students, academics, as well as businesspeople with China experience, interested in modernization and identity, the Chinese perspective, and the new generation of Chinese.

Yunrui Deng was born and raised by a middle-class family in Sichuan Province, Southwest China. She holds a Master of Communication (for Development/Social Change) degree from the University of Queensland, Australia. Fluent in the Sichuan dialect plus bilingual in both English and Mandarin Chinese, she is of the view that it is significant to hear different angles from different generations and backgrounds. Her independent ideas in her first book vis-à-vis identity and modernization provide a unique angle with Western mindset and Chinese reasoning for the international audience as a new generation of Chinese born in the late 1990s. Yunrui's research interests are modernization and identity, Chinese modernization, and communication for development/social change.

A thought-provoking book that looks at the forces of modernity in shaping identity. Having been educated in China and Australia, Yunrui brings a first-hand perspective to the shift in generational norms in China. She has written a must-read book analyzing the forces and differences that have shaped Chinese by different generations. Whether you are an academic or businessperson, the book provides great insight into the shifts in thinking processes and identities in China by generation.

Shaun Rein, *Author of the Split and the End of Cheap China. Founder of the China Market Research Group*

An impressive book that transcends conventional thinking, offering a fresh perspective from China with a global outlook. Yunrui presents a nuanced analysis of modernization and identity, bridging the gap between theory and reality. In our multipolar and multicultural world, it is essential to hear diverse viewpoints from various generations, and this work contributes significantly to that dialogue.

Dr. Seong-Hyon Lee, *Visiting Scholar at Harvard University Asia Center*

In the ever-evolving landscape of our interconnected world, *Beyond Identities in Modernity* stands as a profound narrative, inviting readers to explore the nuanced dynamics of modernization and identity from the unique perspective of a young Chinese intellectual. Yunrui, through her insightful reflections and academic grounding, provides a fresh lens to understand the interplay between East and West and the evolving nature of identities in a globalized world. May Yunrui's authentic words inspire you to look beyond the surface and engage with the deeper currents that shape our modern world.

Fan Hongyi, *Founder of Curidaosity*

An interesting insight from first-hand experience, questioning the importance and impact of identity in shaping one's life journey and choices, especially where cultures have crossed. This account and analysis are all within the context of twenty-first century modernization, such as it is, and very much from the perspective of someone who has lived the experience and sought to identify exactly what her place is in this perceived world.

Jill Scalon, *Board Member of Women in Aid & Development Australia*

Beyond Identities in Modernity

An Outlook Interpreted from a Fresh Chinese Perspective

Yunrui Deng

LONDON AND NEW YORK

First published 2025
by Routledge
4 Park Square, Milton Park, Abingdon, Oxon OX14 4RN

and by Routledge
605 Third Avenue, New York, NY 10158

Routledge is an imprint of the Taylor & Francis Group, an informa business

British Library Cataloguing-in-Publication Data
A catalogue record for this book is available from the British Library

ISBN: 978-1-032-86579-9 (hbk)
ISBN: 978-1-032-86581-2 (pbk)
ISBN: 978-1-003-52818-0 (ebk)

DOI: 10.4324/9781003528180

Typeset in Times New Roman
by KnowledgeWorks Global Ltd.

Contents

Figures and Tables

Figures

Tables

Preface

I neither translate from English to English nor from Chinese to English. I am not from the West. This book, however, is originally composed in English by me. It is a logic grounded in my multicultural education experience and life experience, my personal engagement with people from diverse backgrounds, open data/access from international organizations, excellent readings from thinkers and scholars, as well as my personal micro-observations of this noisy world.

Whenever people in the West talked to me, they often came straight to the point with three questions relating to identity. Where are you from? Which part of China do you come from? Where did you study your English? Anytime my answer was mainland China and Chengdu, I needed to describe the distance between the city in Southwest China and Beijing. They marveled at my liberal, confident, modern, and bilingual nature from an ideologically opposite land whose modernization is not Westernization. If I had not mentioned my origin, people in the West would have presumed that I was born and raised in a Western developed country. I asked whether they had ever been to China, and the majority of them said no.

Australia is a vibrant multicultural country. I attained my Master's degree in Communication (for Development/Social Change) at the University of Queensland in Australia during which an Australian identity was an end that a certain number of people aimed for. An Australian permanent residency identity can spell a permanent stay in this beautiful multicultural nation where myriads of migrants bend over backward to earn an identity by means of constant education, skill match, or even transnational marriage. Every time I chatted with a few temporary residents, a permanent Australian identity was a dream for them to reach the first rung of the so-called Australian society by hook or by crook.

Modernization paradigm was the first communication for development/social change lecture by Associate Professor Pradip Ninan Thomas that I attended at the University of Queensland. I remember Professor Pradip remarked that you knew your country best in terms of your modernization. Modernization theory has led me to observe my micro modernity made in

China and comprehend the changing sense of identities with micro globalization. Then I pondered over identities in modernity. Each time I flipped through books on identity or modernization at bookstores abroad, I discovered that the perspectives were too macro. I felt there were micro gaps that sorely needed to be filled.

I have been fortunate to get acquainted with a handful of well-informed Australian friends who have a good knowledge of the West and China. And one of them asked me and agreed with my views about identity issues at a catchup. I said that recognition was not about for an identity in any modernity, but it was about the demands for dignity and safety. I also think there is a demand for the power of being, and these three elements are beyond identities. During these years, there is apprehension between China and the West hampering people-to-people exchanges. In my opinion, the stereotype is limited to identity bubbles for both peoples. I thereupon formulate this book – *Beyond Identities in Modernity: An Outlook Interpreted from a Fresh Chinese Perspective*.

This is a humane balanced narrative to orbit the micro realities of modernization and globalization that transcend identities by a Chinese born in the late 1990s. This book is not about political economy or social movements, but I draw liberally from a couple of thinkers in the two fields alongside my academic background – communication for development/social change perspectives, to link with micro realities and better present my train of thought to people keen on new angles of modernization and to those who believe in "the end of history." In the twenty-first century's modernization, I am of the view that the young generation of every modernity can be an independent "bridge" between East and West in any sector.

Having read the economist Keyu Jin's *The New China Playbook: Beyond Socialism and Capitalism*, it lights a fire in my mind. I am a member of the cohorts of the new generation of Chinese born in the late 1990s and the first decade of the 2000s, and the new generation is substantially more open-minded and globally conscious than previous generations. I was raised in a middle-class business family. What I have learned from readings and lectures cannot fully speak volumes of my own observations based on pragmatism. As modernization marches on, I think it is significant to hear different angles from different generations and backgrounds. My hope is that my fresh ideas of beyond identities can provide another modern perspective to ultimately conclude an equilibrium of modernization paradigm and better human understanding in this incomprehensible modern world.

Nelson Mandela said, "If you talk to a man in a language he understands, that goes to his head. If you talk to him in his own language, that goes to his heart." Now, *Beyond Identities in Modernity*, if you communicate with the people in a logic they are mesmerized, that goes to their souls. Happy reading.

Acknowledgments

Writing a book is a daunting process, and it involves deep thinking by putting yourself into others' shoes, let alone beyond identities. As a debut author born in the late 1990s from People's Republic of China, this project is both challenging and meaningful for me. It would be the first time that a new generation of Chinese born in the late 1990s has interpreted a modernization outlook in the English language from another unique modern perspective, and ultimately concluded an equilibrium. My belief has sustained me to complete it along the way. All views are totally independent, and the responsibility for errors is mine alone.

First of all, the strong support comes from one's family; my family is my rock. As a UQer, I am indebted to the University of Queensland for the education of knowledge leadership for a better world. I want to thank Associate Professor Pradip Ninan Thomas in the School of Communication and Arts at the University of Queensland, who educated me about modernization paradigm and let me use lecture slides freely in this book. The appreciation also goes to Associate Professor Elske van de Fliert from whom I have learned a lot during Participatory Development Communication classes that have given me a direction to draw the conclusion befitting present and future.

This book would not be possible without the unwavering support of my Commissioning Editor at Routledge, Lucie Bartonek, to whom I owe my deepest gratitude from the beginning. Lucie's faith in me has been essential in the process. The final product could not have been delivered without the kind guidance from Editorial Assistant Bharti Payal. My publisher Routledge Taylor & Francis Group is awesome with spreading knowledge across the globe. I thank everyone's contribution to *Beyond Identities in Modernity*.

China and Australia are very different nations. I would like to acknowledge the Traditional Owners and Custodians of the Aboriginal land across Australia and pay my respect to their Elders' past, present, and emerging, as they have nurtured my thinking in good humanity. I would honor the circular Chinese reasoning that is informed by logic with contexts and a complex system of relationships.

Additionally, shoutout to my friends that offered me time to talk when I was in gloom: Kim Zhu, Fred Liu, Angel Wen, Peter Zhao, Danielle Jane Haratsis, Alvin Yap, Daisy Qin, Beini Liu, and Kalson Yang. To my bestie:

Molly Huili Zhou, many thanks for putting your belief in me and standing by me during every struggle and all my successes. Molly is always my first reader who gives me constructive suggestions. Sandy Qiao, thanks for offering generous assistance when I am in need, you are an exceptional Australian-born Chinese. A thank you goes to Richard with whom I bounced off my fresh ideas on beyond identities over a cup of coffee. Thank you for treating me warmly with British humor and admiring my humble views. I owe you a drink. Grandpa Luo Meifu, thanks for the inspiration of Chinese wisdom.

What makes the book more fantastic is credited to the permissions of publishers, organizations, and individuals that grant the material use – John Wiley & Sons, Simon & Schuster, Profile Books, UQ Library, Pew Research Center, OECD org, the United Nations, Institute of Development Studies, and Eli De Friend. I do hope readers around the world can benefit the knowledge in this book just as those writers and thinkers that have sparked my thinking over the years.

Introduction

I am from the world's second-largest economy in the modern twenty-first century. Precisely, I am steeped in Southwest China – Sichuan Province, home to over 80 million people, a basin which sits on the eastern part of Tibetan Plateau, the Yungui Plateau to the south, and the central Chengdu Plain. This Southwestern inland soil is fertile with slow-paced life and the hilarious regional dialect notwithstanding lagging behind all-around development. The dynastic cycle of Chinese civilization remains a presence recognizing where I stem from and how history may yet be the death of me. Stretching as far as 9.6 million square kilometers from the northernmost tip Mohe city to the southernmost tip Nansha Islands, China is large and is constantly changing. It is believed that the future of China will be a key stage in the twenty-first century for the rest of the world. The eyes are riveted on the new generation of Chinese. Contrary to modernization theory, Chinese modernization is an odd against modernization theorists by whom I was trained in the West. The public discourse is inundated with the good and the bad modern events with the acceleration of globalization. The biggest question in the twenty-first century is not about who will dominate the world touting a new world order upon us. Rather, the orientation of modernization is the biggest question that haunts our daily realities.

This is a book reaching beyond identities penned by a young Chinese born in the late 1990s. Identity and modernization are interrelated albeit Francis Fukuyama's declaration on "the end of history." With Western references particularly Francis Fukuyama, this book mainly argues against identity for recognition but for dignity, safety, and the power of being. The American anthropologist Edward T. Hall's work *Beyond Culture* presents a thorough anthropological voyage in the twentieth century that helps us rethink our different cultures to better understand other people. As time goes by, I think we should go beyond identities in the twenty-first century. So, what does beyond identities mean?

I am not suggesting universalism. "The end of history" is a clue that examines where modernization is going. It has been frequently explored by

DOI: 10.4324/9781003528180-1

writers in the West for identity per se and the monotonous modernization model with a macro lens. Beyond identities, is for sure, an odd. We cannot deny that there is a kaleidoscope of identities in this day and age, and identities are dynamic with our lived experience. A hidden truth is that we are humans hankering after dignity, safety, and the power of being. And the three aspects alter with identities. At this stage, communication technologies have provoked overwhelming identity shifts within modernization paradigm, and this rise above identities over space. And the vicissitudes of globalization strikingly make people closer to each other. We are aware that there is not less than one modernization model throughout the world. Regardless of identities, at last, beyond identities intends to pick up an outlook of modernization with micro realities articulated by a member of the new generation of Chinese from another modern perspective so that we can better understand each other and sum up an equilibrium of modernization befitting present and future.

The modernization outlook interpretation is a blend of my Chinese identity rooted in Southwest China and my Western multicultural education involvement in Australia. It is an angle with both Western mindset and Chinese reasoning that a Chinese international student independently presents. Chinese identity for me is an accumulation of the native Chinese language, China's expansive natural landscapes, extensive ancient imperial wisdom, as well as hundreds of Chinese foods. This is my land. And being Chinese for me is a sovereignty over every inch of rivers and mountains. Time ticking away, a startling wave of China's modern economic miracle and technological advancement has shaped a Chinese identity in the eyes of the new generation. Unlike the previous generations, being part of the new generation of Chinese is a process of modernizing identities and a progress of changing sense of identities with micro-globalization.

This book begins with tracing identity politics as part of Western modernization. Identity politics shapes social change despite its contentious development. The declaration of "the end of history" expects modern Western society to supplant others, which implies that identity politics will grow all over such modernization. For a long time, recognition has been a banner of identity, so the American political scientist Francis Fukuyama comes up with the idea that modern Western society is a process of *isothymia* over *megalothymia* driven by a struggle of recognition-based identities in reference to Hegel's philosophy. Modernization theory has been in essence propounded by thinkers from the West – whether it is about the correlation between economic growth and democracy or the desire for Westernization worldwide.

However, one size does not fit all, and China's modernization is not Westernization. The unique model is more officially called "modernization with Chinese characteristics," but the elaboration of the economist Keyu Jin in *The New China Playbook: Beyond Socialism and Capitalism* has got across the view that the paternalistic modernity makes room for creative local business and the improvement of standard of living under political centralization married to economic decentralization of the mayor economy.

The micro-level of modernization in China on modernizing identities is fascinating for the new generation of Chinese. A Chinese household living in "modernization with Chinese characteristics" can possess over 30 percent saving rate of income on average, while a counterpart in the West is below 10 percent (figures are compiled by OECD.org in Chapter 1). Chinese middle-class families support the financial expenses of Chinese international students that gigantically contribute to the economic development of Western developed countries. In consequence, Chinese international students can soak up Western soft power and a radically different worldview that reshape their identities within modernization paradigm according to "transnational identity" term. Of course, Chinese modernization will not be Westernized because it is a paternalistic modernity with unbalanced Western contacts among the Chinese people. By utilizing theories and research, Chapter 1 is a narrative on Another Understanding of Identities, coming to know about modernizing identities in relation to my personal modern journey and the changing sense of identities with micro-globalization. I am modernized. I share a nuanced view that is off the books. There are several macro contentions shadowing a right micro view, so all too often a lot of noise eclipses the down-to-earth micro realities.

Lots of us are obsessed with identity building, and we acknowledge that the power of identity lies in its ability to foster individuals' actions and relationships as well as to influence the operation of a society at large. Chapter 2 is related to the power of identity; it is written by reviewing *The Power of Identity* by the Spanish sociologist Manuel Castells and breaking the code of identity terms combined with my observation of beyond identities from the micro realities within modernization paradigm. Understanding the power of identity is indispensable to going beyond identities. We will check out the very widespread network society moves beyond identities, affecting social contract in guanxi behavior (a type of Chinese social networking) and weak ties (a type of Western social networking). One way or another, Manuel Castells' point of view on three types of identities concerning social movements has enlightened me to look beyond identities.

We all have a *legitimizing identity* that validates individuals to be participants in micro-globalization. No matter where your origin is, *legitimizing identity* brings legitimacy by shoring up migration programs, vaccination campaigns, and national holidays. A *resistance identity* is incompatible with traditional values and legitimizing identities. Technological change penetrates identity redefinition in the twenty-first century, and a far-reaching possibility is for women's reproduction of parenthood contrary to the deep-seated patriarchalism around the world. The ensuing effects of this resistance identity are vital to future generations. Although there may not be a tangible global identity, *project identity* develops with the diffusion of global inflows of economy and information. The powerful objective of project identities is to transform a society. The case of Net Zero 2050, or Sustainable Development Goals, projects a brand-new identity against the challenges of Mother Nature facing humankind to defend the Earth and human well-being.

If we continue to classify identity itself, it is unlikely to transcend identities. Migration is an incredible movement in modernity along with globalization. The common conviction is that the decision to move appertains to establishing one's identity. Multiculturalism flourishes beyond identities. In Chapter 3, we will read beyond identities through the internal migration in China, international migration, as well as multiculturalism in Australia. I collect available open data and research analysis from international organizations that are managing the contemporary migration picture. The consequences of international migration are the outcomes of macro policies around the world, propelling in-group competition among migrants and business organizations. The economic and social consequences can be double-edged sword for both host societies and home societies. To be better is on the hunt for opportunities that villages and traditional societies do not offer, and it is at the core of modern human demands. In the context of globalization, everyone has become more diversified than ever in each modernity. To this point, modernization and identity are open to globalization.

The thesis in this book is that the real intentions behind identities as humankind aim to modern dignity and safety, and the power of being in modernity. Chapter 4 is in prose style, which contains a philosophical narrative predicated on daily realities that are subject to philosophy. Dignity and safety are the interaction of the three varieties of knowledge of our minds, other minds, and external realities, as we will see in Chapter 4. Identity can be a limited trade-off for one's dignity and safety under the influence of identity economics. I draw from the book *Identity Economics* collaborated by the American economists Rachel Kranton and George Akerlof in favor of identity utility. We should never lose sight of the viability of hard work rewards regardless of the diversity of a society. What I focus on is and will always be the people-centered micro everyday observation. Most importantly, dreams are associative dignity and safety. We know that macro dreams make people dream big; in some senses, macro dreams meet nothing less than micro dreams for a better tomorrow.

Modernization underlies the power of being. It changes social relationships and values yet power relationships. Chapter 5 proposes that where there is identity, there is power. Identities, in a way, anchor the power for modern dignity and safety. It presents a view that power relations drive humankind to progress in dignity and safety instead of recognition. As claimed by Manuel Castells, "whoever has power shapes the institutions that regulate society in terms of its interests and values." Regardless of identities, the power of being is run after by each individual far and wide in every disparate modernity. It argues that the power of being resides in power relationships in all domains of our everyday realities. As such, Chapter 5 concurs with the French philosopher Michel Foucault's thought on micro-powers that power is what makes us what we are. By discussing "knowledge is power," the maxim evolves with modernization and identity for whom and for what. What's more, the nuanced understanding of the power of being is closely linked to the complicated exercise of power through the lens of the "power cube." The "power cube" approach by the political sociologist John Gaventa suggests that the participation of power and powerlessness amplifies inequality to the concentration of economic wealth vis-à-vis political power. For this, the power of being is concerned with participation. Leaving political considerations aside, the lens of the "power cube" of Chapter 5 in this beyond identities book explores these three topics – economic empowerment, education, communication – based on power relationships with relevance to modernization paradigm.

Modernization paradigm accentuates economic accumulation. This is essential to macro-globalization and micro individual desires for modern dignity and safety. As we recover from the COVID-19 global pandemic, economies are grappling with tough uncertainties in respect of slowdown, inflation, unemployment, and cost-of-living pressures. The analysis in this beyond identities book concludes an equilibrium for an outlook of modernization from a communication for development/social change perspective. "The end of history" does not stand up any longer as we will read "modernization with Chinese characteristics" in Chapter 1 and participatory modernization in Chapter 6. In today's multicultural world, this equilibrium of modernization is about participation in every aspect of modernization powered by communication technologies from the third decade onward in the twenty-first century. Yet, participation will not become a paradigm and replace modernization paradigm. I call this equilibrium as the participatory modernization framework of modernization paradigm. There are understandably radical divergences between East and West in modern times. An inspiration from Confucianism tells us harmony in diversity (和而不同he er bu tong) or seeking common ground while reserving differences (求同存异 qiu tong cun yi). This can be achieved as indicated by participatory development communication. In Chapter 6, we will read that the participatory modernization framework grows with the short video economy, despite the fact that censorship exists in a few societies. The restrictions of censorship vary from high-context cultures to low-context cultures. It is a test for each modernity's moral and cultural norms within modernization paradigm. Also, we must be good to collaboratively coping with the drawbacks of modernization such as pollution, climate change, mental health, and inequalities by means of participation. Whatever modernization heads to, power relations drive humankind's history to be modern dignity and safety.

Postmodernity is incongruent with the realities because the stages of modernization are still antithetical to each other in some parts of the world considering the Indigenous population. Future generations are already born into a modernized era. The history of future generations will be both rather thrilling and uncontrollable at a time when communication technologies are poised to manipulate children's desires for entertainment, education, and their identities. Last but not least, competition remains ongoing for macro modernization in all societies when future generations choose their dignity and safety.

I do not write a book about an adherent of focus in imagination. It is interdisciplinary and down-to-earth. I use theories, data, and even philosophy as toolboxes to align with micro realities around you and me. The data are open access from international organizations. This book is not on China albeit a set of China cases. Witnessing Chinese modernization, identities, and the world from China and in Australia beyond day by day, I provide a more suitable, more pragmatic, and possibly, more nuanced perspective.

Between East and West, between theories and realities, and between macro and micro, thinking through modernization and identity calls for going beyond the mere paradigm, rising above conventional wisdom, as well as hearing different angles from different generations and backgrounds. Only by fully grasping beyond identities with its intricate and often contradictory dynamics can we truly discuss modernization paradigm. Only then can we critique modernization and identity intelligently – both recognizing the merits and identifying the challenges, then pointing out a way forward.

May this book will make the noisy modern world a more peaceful and humane place until my "end of history." To readers interested in modernization and identity, I have tried to share another modern perspective of reaching beyond identities; otherwise, few have provided. To readers observing China, I am convinced that it is far more important to hear the down-to-earth micro realities expressed by different generations and backgrounds. To people who pursue identity, I am hopeful that achieving another modern perspective of beyond identities will help to better achieve identity. Please read on.

1 Another Understanding of Identities

What is identity? The dictionary definitions translate the word: (a) the distinguishing character or personality of an individual, (b) the facts or information of being a person, and (c) the sameness between reality and an object. "Identity" is an ordinary word, but the knowledge concerning identity is extraordinary in an array of disciplines. Notably, the American psychologist Erik Erikson proposes that the psychosocial evolution of identity constitutes the entire life stage characterized by conflicts. In other words, identity cannot separate identity crisis when one's role changes.[1]

I know going beyond identities would be a complex narrative because identities are not simply related to nationality, language, culture, religion, race, gender, sexual orientation, and social class. Identities are dynamic with our lived experience. The process of modernization, globalization, and social movements in each nation mold us into heterogeneous identities. Spurred by social mobility, diversity has become a fact of life and a value, no matter what polity advances development agendas. As the interactions of different communities grow, identities are manifested in that idea of identity politics.

The term "identity politics" has explained a collection of groups that seek their interests and facilitate actions based upon identity categories or social roles since at least the modern 1970s. Fast forward to today's twenty-first century, the scope of identity politics appears to creep into every aspect of life defined by identity. The traditional national identity can be repurposed to fit public discourse for media consumption; however, a wide variety of identities project the aspirations of human beings into economic satisfaction, career opportunities, better life quality, and decent social welfare as such. Within identities, the marginalized identities feel powerless against mainstream identities and advocate for equality; other identities are further boosted by communication process, learning experience, and external factors throughout life, be they elites or ordinary people.

This book is not to expand on identity politics for there have been a vast number of professionals writing mountains of work with regard to the past and the present of identity politics. But it begins with identity politics communication for readers to understand the relevance of identity. In this chapter,

DOI: 10.4324/9781003528180-2

I will trace identity politics, introduce a partial knowledge of recognition for identity, and frame modernizing identities for the new generation of Chinese in relation to my personal modern journey. At the same time, I will connect the changing sense of identities with micro-globalization in Chinese modernization.

Tracing Identity Politics

You may feel "identity politics" is a strong notion when it springs to your mind. More often than not, our weird fast thinking fosters an understanding of words and behaviors. At first glance, identity politics may sound like radicalism. Well, this is a superficial comprehension of identity politics.

Granted, many of identity activities are associated with communities from minorities, immigrants, Indigenous people, gays, lesbians, and feminists struggling for their own demands that are not on the same page with authorities. By emphasizing the disagreements between these communities and political institutions, identities are naturally colored as political-related events. Throughout social sciences and humanities, identity politics functions as a descriptive phrase that applies to movements characterized by various identities. The sociological analyses thereby could develop identity politics relevant to our different societies reflective of race, religion, family, or class.[2]

Chronologically, the roots of identity politics go back to the late eighteenth century and early nineteenth century when counter-Enlightenment attacked the idea of universalism and advocated that each human identity could be defined by distinctive biological, social, and moral characteristics. Sentiments of anti-Enlightenment universalism were expressed across European societies with Romantics favoring cultural differences in identities. In doing so, the cultural spirit acted as the cultural forerunner of racial typologies that shaped Western thought between the nineteenth and early twentieth centuries. In the wake of the Second World War, it took two decades for identity politics to revive. The late 1960s and 1970s have witnessed increased movements of the underrepresented groups themed women, immigration, and ethnicity that focused on equality outcomes in America, including Black Civil Rights Movement, Second Wave Feminism, and Sexual Liberation.[3] The modern name identity politics was coined by the American Combahee River Collective in 1977, a black lesbian organization, which argued that the politics of identity takes people's experiences at the center of struggles. Over decades, the phrase "identity politics" has become a force in Western public life with concentrations on both large-scale identities and particular individuals. The left-right spectrum promotes respective demand for the interests of multicultural groups and traditional national identity protection under the umbrella of identity. The demands pertaining to identities vary from more economic redistribution to greater freedom.[4]

I came across "the rise of identity politics" from Francis Fukuyama's interpretation when I was studying for my Master's degree in Communication for Development/Social Change at the University of Queensland in Australia. The philosophy of identity politics is imported from the West. I have immersed myself into this multicultural nation while learning about the Indigenous people of Australia, engaging in daily life with locals and immigrants, and observing campaigns such as the Voice to Parliament and Reconciliation Week. Technically, I am an outsider despite the around 5.5 percent of Chinese heritage in the Australian population. Acculturation has advanced my language level, liberal thinking, and the Western way of life. The minor identity politics that plays out in communities – whether national, ethnic, religious, sexual, or gender – could be revolving around identities.

The ever-narrower identities turn their desires into collective demands by groups as a whole in modernity: the workers' unions gather together to urge pay rise; the Indigenous people demonstrate on the street to claim sovereignty over their lands; immigrants from China, India, Greece, Japan, and so forth launch initiatives to push forward with their community agendas; and environmentalists organize climate change action for the journey to net zero. Straddling between my Chinese identity and Western liberalism, I see an essential component beyond the cravings of these identities of being modern – that is dignity. I will illustrate modern dignity and safety in relation to philosophy with my views in Chapter 4. It could demand that organizations alleviate the cost-of-living pressures and enhance financial power for working people, or it could demand power of lands for the Indigenous population, or it could demand efforts to cope with burdens of invisibility, disrespect, and recognition for immigrants, or it could demand harmonious relationship with nature.

As such, identity politics is changeable with our modern identities. Some perceive their identities fixed on biology and country; others have multiple identities nurtured by social interactions that facilitate collective engagement. Identity politics develops societies into small segments that run public agendas. In a sense, identity terms are like wheels to drive social change.

Recognition for Identity

In *the End of History and the Last Man* by the American political scientist Francis Fukuyama, it was expected that modern Western society would spread globally as a last form of social order.[5] With this logic, if so, my assumption is that identity politics would grow in the Westernized social order because identity politics originates from the West as part of Western modernization. This growth of identity politics in the Western world carries its weight in the repurposing of identity, which inspires each individual's self. Identity as a motivator of social movements is valued in three types analyzed by the Spanish sociologist Manuel Castells, this accounts for the power of identity in the network society. We will explore the three types of identities in Chapter 2. However, we may have an identity based on recognition. This view sounds one-dimensional. It is still necessary to have knowledge of the one-dimensional identity based on recognition.

The word "recognition" is used in plenty of contexts to identify and acknowledge a person's existence, merits, or accomplishments. It indicates the right to be heard and given attention, so "acknowledgement" and "recognition" are used interchangeably. Recognition is also extended to public discourse when a nation would like to demonstrate respect for other people or government. For example, an Acknowledgement of Country in Australia is usually delivered as a sign of respect for the traditional custodians of the land on which a meeting or event is being held, meaning the continuing relationship between Aboriginal and Torres Strait Islander peoples and the country.

There is a considerable body of work in philosophy on the issue of recognition. Browsing through the previous writings by Immanuel Kant, Axel Honneth, Marcel Proust, Thomas Hobble, and Hegel, the contemporary French philosopher Paul Ricoeur has deciphered "to recognize" and "to identify" throughout the important book *The Course of Recognition* that recognition is a deep discussion moving from language to memory in recognizing oneself and mutual recognition. In Ricoeur's view, the forms of love, universal respect, and social esteem give a place to the struggle for recognition that is held in Hegelian conception. The social recognition is endless through certificates, relationships, as well as identity politics.[6]

In the modern West, the Canadian philosopher Charles Taylor argues that modernity not only demands a politics of equal dignity but also a politics of difference in *The Politics of Recognition* that reflects identity politics.[7] In Dr. Catherine Monnet's *Recognition the Key to Identity*, the main thesis states that without recognition, we will not have a consciousness of self and develop sound relationships with others. Recognition is existentially important to interpret our behaviors to build identity through the mirror of others being liked on social media, complimented on appearance, and applauded for our work.[8]

Human beings are motivated by a sort of desire for material goods and inner fulfillment, including food, water, shelter, clothing, self-actualization, love, and belonging. Reason directs the need in the form of desire to some extent. Further, *thymos* (English: *thumos*) complements decision-making as a means of recognition, which Francis Fukuyama stands up for the spirit of identity. *Thumos* means self-perception is on the basis of identification by society, and it is elaborated in two expressions from Francis Fukuyama's perspective. The first is called "megalothymia" – for a desire to be superior to others. *Megalothymia* is pursued in the roles of political power, C-suites, senior managers, top elites, show stars, etc. The other is called "isothymia" – for people who want to be recognized as equally good as everyone in society. *Isothymia* is associated with the beliefs of belonging, equality, humanism, solidarity, etc. For Francis Fukuyama, modern Western society is a process of *isothymia* over *megalothymia* driven by a struggle of identities.[9] It seems to be plausible that recognition for identity allows human soul to promote justice and satisfy internal pride. Drawing upon the German philosopher Georg Wilhelm Friedrich Hegel, Francis Fukuyama believes that recognition-based identities have driven humankind to progress leading to a modern Western liberal society.

Recognition can be straightforward for identity to lift up feel-good slogans in a wide range of social movements such as Reconciliation and Yes/No Vote. Without generational shift, the discourse has been narrowly focused on the Western ideas of identity and modern society that try to equate modernization with Westernization. Born and raised in China, educated in both China and the West, I reckon that Chinese modernization is the other way around. My micro-observations about identities within modernization paradigm go beyond identities.

Modernizing Identities for the New Generation of Chinese

The evolution of modernization often brings up Karl Max's quote, "It is slavery which has given their value to the colonies, it is the colonies which have created the commerce of the world, it is the commerce of the world which is the essential condition of the great industry. Thus, slavery is an economic category of the highest importance."[10] That was how slavery and colonization wrote the history of modernization. In the nineteenth century, Britain became the preeminent creation of modernization in many colonial societies, pouring commercial expansion into various independent societies.

For all practical purposes, modernization theory has been the reigning theory in development for more than half a century. Modernization is premised upon a binary opposition between tradition and modernity. It is a liberalism's theory that contributes to the process of change. Similarly, modernization paradigm was restructured between the 1950s and 1960s after the Second World War. Modernization theory sought to create all facets of human achievements in society whose concepts were primarily fleshed out by scholars in the West.[11] The American economist Walt Rostow brought modernization theory to prominence in the book *The Stages of Economic Growth*. Walt Rostow echoed the five stages of economic modernization's varying length – traditional society, preconditions for take-off, take-off, drive to maturity, and high mass consumption. He formulated that an economy would take off once it had reached a critical stage. This critical stage would be characterized by a rise in the rate of productive investment, the development of a manufacturing sector, and the emergence of a balanced socio-economic and political structure, which would lead to take off and growth.[12] Furthermore, the American sociologist and political scientist Seymour Martin Lipset was a key proponent of modernization theory – economic growth sets in motion multifaceted social changes, including urbanization, industrialization, wealth, and education that are prerequisites for democracy.[13]

In the book *The Passing of Traditional Society: Modernizing the Middle East*, the American scholar Daniel Lerner constructed the modernization model according to which exposure to communication and mass media of US products played a dominant role in speeding up economic and social development.[14] After the Second World War, modernization as a discourse is normally led by the American version writ large. In other words, if the American way could be copied globally, foreigners would become more like Americans and desire to Westernize. In this regard, education and mass media are agents trickling down new ideas and innovations to the Third World. At the end of the day, to be modern is supposed to be better than traditional.[15]

A number of realities have been contradictions to the simple causal modernization paradigm. For example, economic growth can be bolstered in a variety of ways and directions that tend to conceptualize one's modernity. Although modernization theorists consider tradition as a barrier to modernization, I deem this does not mean identities will not change. When modernization diffuses new inventions over old practices, our identities undoubtedly would be modernized. In the meantime, my thinking is that modernizing identities is not the same as identity politics. The modern journey of the new generation of Chinese is another modern narrative.

I come from China, a vast nation with 56 ethnic minorities and widely varying landscapes, where 1.4 billion people have become modernized in a stunningly short amount of 30 years facilitated by the macro opening up since 1978. Without a full-fledged colonization of any Western societies in Chinese history, "modernization with Chinese characteristics" is generally unusual, fast, and peaceful, which has delivered tremendous benefits to both rural families and urban families. None of the assumptions of modernization theory can truly narrate "modernization with Chinese characteristics" in the matter of a correlation between China's economic miracle and the modern Chinese behaviors in reality.

The New China Playbook: Beyond Socialism and Capitalism by the Chinese economist Keyu Jin has clearly illustrated that the distinctive feature of "modernization with Chinese characteristics" is political centralization paired with economic decentralization of mayor economy whose local officials are committed to expanding from economic growth to foreign investment, from international cultural events to global talents through regional initiatives so as to climb up to higher positions which essentially rest on the local economy's performance.

To most outsiders, "modernization with Chinese characteristics" may sound both dominating and mind-blowing. But the Chinese life has come a long way. Thanks to the hardworking struggle of the earlier generations, the young generation of Chinese, such as super-educated me and my peers born in the late 1990s and after 2000, is able to enjoy a relatively comfortable life, study abroad, and see the world. As indicated by *The Stages of Economic Growth*, people not only save more with an increase of income yielded from the expansion in the modern sectors but also place savings to engage in modern activities.[16] The burgeoning of the Chinese middle classes assiduously saves and supports the new generation of Chinese to become much more open-minded, creative, assertive, and educated.

The post-1990s and post-2000s social cohorts of my generation are the typical vanguards of China's one-child policy. As most Chinese families have only one child under the influence of this policy, the majority of this new generation enjoys over-investment from older generations. The most noteworthy mention of "modernization with Chinese characteristics" is that Chinese families devote 25 percent of annual spending to a child's education on average.[17] This is a far more astronomical cost than most families in Western modernization. In many aspects, China is far from a rich developed country; however, Chinese households set aside an average of more than 30 percent of disposable income over the last two decades as Keyu Jin notes, making China one of the highest saving rates in the world.[18] The average saving propensity of a Chinese family stands in contrast to Western households compiled by OECD.org as of 2019 (See Table 1.1) – about 7.5 percent in America, 12 percent in Australia, −0.7 percent in the United Kingdom, 2 percent or so in Canada, and many other countries are below 10 percent.[19]

In light of modernization theory, economic development would fuel better education and further shift values and social relationships. This is true for the new generation of Chinese, especially Chinese international students who have got exposure to Western modernization. Statista shows that more than 700,000 Chinese students went abroad for overseas studies in 2019, with an increase of 6.25 percent compared to 2018.[20] Interestingly, the funding of Chinese international students is produced by "modernization with Chinese characteristics" that totally clashes with modernization theorists, whereas the economic development of Western developed countries is boosted by the education spending of the modern young Chinese.

The annual income generated by Chinese international students is worth over 10 billion Australian dollars for the Australian economy, over 5 billion

Table 1.1 Average household savings of disposable household income 2009–2019 in Australia, United Kingdom, United States, Canada, and China

Year	*Australia*	*United Kingdom*	*United States*	*Canada*	*China*
2009	5.6%	5.6%	6.1%	4.5%	37.7%
2010	7.4%	6.8%	6.5%	4.3%	38.5%
2011	7.9%	4%	7%	4.2%	38%
2012	6.5%	3.1%	8.9%	4.7%	38.2%
2013	7.4%	2.8%	6.3%	4.7%	37.8%
2014	7.6%	1.7%	7.3%	3.5%	36.8%
2015	6.1%	4.2%	7.8%	4.1%	35.7%
2016	5.5%	0.6%	7.2%	1.6%	34.6%
2017	4.9%	−0.7%	7.5%	1.9%	34.4%
2018	5.7%	−0.8%	7.8%	0.7%	34.8%
2019	12.2%	−0.7%	7.5%	1.9%	34.4%

Source: Adapted from the data compiled by OECD. Household savings (indicator). 2023. doi: 10.1787/cfc6f499-en (Accessed on 26 August 2023). The figures during COVID-19 in some countries were nil.

pounds contribution to the UK economy, more than 14 billion US dollars to the US economy, and about 5 billion US dollars to Canada's economy.[21] Following "transnational identity" term, people who have multicultural living experiences between home and host societies will re-establish and modify mixed senses of belonging, intercultural competence, and social cognitive intimacy between home and host societies.[22] Hence, in return, Chinese international students can absorb new ideas and a completely different worldview that reshape their identities within modernization paradigm. In this aspect, foreign international students are not the key source of national revenue in the Chinese economy.

Growing up with "modernization with Chinese characteristics," the new generation of Chinese (Generation Z) has been instructed to learn the English language in the third grade since primary school. English is a compulsory subject from grade three in China officially introduced by China's Ministry of Education since 2003.[23] Even though the English educational approach in China rigidly stresses rote learning and test-taking, there are estimated around 400 million Chinese people learning English, larger than the entire population of all Western nations.[24] Today, English learning in China begins at an earlier age in kindergarten; in the meantime, tons of English private tutoring schools play a critical role in liberating the younger generation within the framework of "modernization with Chinese characteristics" other than making a fortune. What's more, the push for English learning is of significant importance in Chinese higher education. There are more than 300 English major programs nationwide in Chinese modernization provided by international studies universities, comprehensive universities, as well as normal universities and teachers' colleges.[25] The two main strands are – non-English major learners can take English as an elective course and must pass College English Test Bands Four and Six (CET-4 and CET-6) during college days; English major learners must pass CET 4 and 6, as well as Test for English Majors Bands Four and Eight (TEM-4 and TEM-8).

The 2020 findings from Chinese Academy of Social Sciences demonstrated that 47 percent of the post-1990s generation had access to higher education, and almost 96 percent and 74 percent of the post-1990s generation had completed junior high school and high school, respectively. A higher proportion can be expected for the group of the post-2000s generation.[26] In Chinese modernization, every new generation of Chinese bears the shadow of the struggle with make-or-break Gaokao, the annual college entrance exam, that stratifies the society under the influence of its imperial examination system. In a country where getting a degree is required to obtain a good job, a Chinese endures twelve years of cramming only for the three-day exam called Gaokao. No matter how open the Chinese are, Gaokao remains a serious national experience for many Chinese.

Indeed, education is a transformative agent to modernize us. I am no exception. Education and communication have turned me into a modern liberal human being just as the Brazilian educator Paulo Freire put an emphasis on

Conscientization, referring to an individual who develops a critical consciousness and understanding of social reality through reflection and action.[27]

Flashing back to the late 1990s, I was born in Qiuxi Town, a small town approximately 78 miles (125 km) away from the provincial capital city Chengdu. The intensive water network in Sichuan Province branches off the Yangtze River and nourishes the lives of its people, and thereby Qiuxi Town was built along the Qiuxi River during the reign of Emperor Jia Qing of the Qing Dynasty (circa 1796–1820). Due to modern China's household registration system (hukou), my identity belonged to the non-agricultural category (commonly referred to as urban), which was with my paternal family. My maternal family was from a rural village belonging to the agricultural household. Qiuxi Town was my archaic history in the early 2000s with no mobile phone and the Internet, and I had no inkling of the outside world. In Qiuxi Town, a tiny color television and a corded home phone had been my communication life by 2003, and my family pulled out all the stops to save and do small businesses by selling smallware for a living. The Market Days during weekdays were boisterous with people across villages when businesses could make a small fortune. At that time, our life was hard up for tomorrow's opportunities in the small town. By the time I started elementary school in 2004, my mother was eager to seek better education for me with economic liberalism in mind. Thus, my family moved to Ziyang City, a prefecture-level city bordered by the provincial capital city Chengdu to the northeast, where I spent most of my time in China.

In 2004, we also purchased our first home-grown flip phone only used for calling and texting at the cost of about 140 US dollars. Soon I was exposed to computers, cellphones, infrastructures, schools, and the English language that have made me better than traditional. My knowledge about the world has never ceased, and my middle-class family worked hard and saved for my overseas education. As the economic condition of my family prospered with business, we were gradually moving to Chengdu, the provincial capital city, where I call my current home in China. Consequently, the individual efforts basically empower the dignity and safety of my modern journey. By the dignity and safety of my modern journey, I mean one's modern life is an arduous process through hard work to be better for the sake of basic survival needs, self-love, education, and resources, which has nothing to do with modernization theory. The story of Chinese modernization is a story of rapid change. This modern dignity and safety in Chinese modernity for me and the new generation of Chinese households have taken place just within a single generation owing to the macro opening up practice and the micro persistent saving endeavors.

Economic development has been pivotal to modernizing our life demands, and the experiences of education and communication emancipate our traditional values or even change social relationships. For this, the identities are modernized. Zakary Dychtwald, the author of *Young China*, describes a cogent portrait of Chinese millennials nurtured in "modernization with Chinese characteristics"– the Chinese younger generation who are well educated and traveled widely shows a more open attitude to everything not to mention sex compared with their Western counterparts living in Western modernization. The majority of China's new generation has not been Westernized, but they are modernized with Chinese characteristics while admiring the progressive Western things.[28]

As I see it, modernization theory develops with identity politics in society, but modernization theory fails to explain the individual experiences of modernizing identities for the new generation in China. Personally, my identity is more than legitimizing Chinese. The Chinese language enables me to learn about deep connotations that are rooted in traditional Chinese values. The bilingual proficiency in the English language and knowledge of another German language gift me opportunities to engage with a larger world. Chinese dishes are brain food for me to enhance my sense of belonging to China and to understand the subcultures of different regions. I also enjoy other Western-style meals and Asian foods such as Aussie Brunch, American fast food, British tea, Vietnamese Pho, Thai Curry Beef, Indonesian Grilled Fish, Japanese Sushi, and South Korean Hot Pot. Australian education has encouraged me to take initiative and apply knowledge leadership for a better world while I appreciate the Chinese education system with an emphasis on perseverance, discipline, and knowledge as well. Wider, I have been intrigued by European civilization that enlightened movements around the world. So, this is modernizing identities. The Chinese modernization maintains its own approach with Western exposure among the new generation.

The Changing Sense of Identities with Micro-globalization

The author of *The World is Flat*, Thomas L. Friedman, sensed the inevitability of a fast change through globalization and updated economic concepts in 2005. As a strong advocate for free trade, Friedman proposed that countries, companies, and individuals needed to remain competitive in globalization.[29] That being said, identity shifts with globalization have been underrated, in particular with micro-globalization.

Identity has been a ubiquitous globalized discourse that escapes the definition of identity. We are still undergoing the process of modernization, but globalization is an extension of modernization. Globalization goes beyond time, place, and space, within which the compression of the world and connections among people are accelerated by digital communication. Looking back on history, the First Industrial Revolution and the Second Industrial Revolution aided by steamships, trains, cars, as well as planes have left a mark on every member of each society since the middle of the eighteenth century.[30] The view of macro-globalization stresses large-scale cross-border trade, financial transactions, supply chains, and cultural diffusion – the circulation and interdependence are overall derived from economic globalization.[31]

Speaking of micro-globalization, my thought is focused on people-oriented interactions worldwide with products, travel, education, and electronic communication that redefine the sense of identities over the first half of my modern lifespan. Micro-globalization is based on ordinary people. The methodology of micro-globalization concerns local dwellers who consume, communicate, and connect beyond boundaries.[32] The new generation of Chinese is in tandem with a transformative of value system stimulated by a wave of micro-globalization. The conditions of micro-globalization can, to an extent, bring about a dramatic generational gap in values differing from the older Chinese generations who did not grow up in the era of opening up "modernization with Chinese characteristics."[33]

In my memory, by 2005, international mobile phone giants such as Samsung, Sony, Nokia, and Motorola were impressive in the Chinese market on out-of-home advertisements. As a child, I wished to be one of these global fancy phone consumers. A significant tool for me to participate in micro-globalization kicked off with the English language in 2007 when my mother signed up for after-school English courses because of my interest and my aspiration to study abroad. Foreign language learning is certainly critical to modernizing identities for the new generation of Chinese. It is more about learning a fresh pattern of thinking. It is a way to unlock another self-potential. Later, the first iPhone was released in the United States in 2007, and it came out in China in 2009. In my eyes, the first decade of the twenty-first century was an infancy of the changing sense of identities with micro-globalization for the new generation of Chinese.

Increasingly, a mix of dizzying progress was interwoven with the second-largest economic power and technology in the second decade of the twenty-first century. At a time when technology platforms recreated everything from hailing a taxi to our most intimate relations, the intense global competition between Chinese companies and foreign firms has diversified the lives of Chinese people. A smartphone cannot be a luxury any longer, and the Chinese market is full of both innovative native manufacturers such as Huawei, Xiaomi, Oppo and established foreign brands like Apple and Samsung. A smartphone is at the center of behavior changes from digital payments to messaging on Alipay and WeChat.

When it comes to the free flow of people, the number of Chinese outbound trips reached approximately 131 million as of 2017, and McKinley & Company pointed out that China was still the world's largest outbound travel market measured by trips and expenditures.[34] Chinese consumers take in French wines, Australian beef, New Zealand milk, American films, and a host of other imported commodities, and the Chinese people are free to join networking events, cultural exchanges, and panel discussions with foreigners. At the time expats go grocery shopping at Sam's Club, Carrefour, or Auchan in China, they are in awe of a collection of Western brands that are available for the Chinese people queuing up in the non-Westernized "modernization with Chinese characteristics."

Labeled as globalization-based acculturation, exposure to a set of foreign cultural streams selectively chooses identities from various worldviews via channels such as media, trade, education, and tourism.[35] The micro-globalization actions implicate a string of identity shifts of social and cultural connections between original identity and Western destinations.[36] On this basis, I see the second decade of the twenty-first century as an accelerator of the changing sense of identities with micro-globalization for the new generation of Chinese. This means a national identity is becoming more embedded in the immense advancement of digital technology, global connectivity, as well as Western soft power. During the phenomenal second decade, my life in Southwest China was characterized by digitalization, international travel, and global brands consumption, which I had never anticipated in my childhood. Subsequently, the Chinese identity has possessed a global awareness, a global reference, and an ability to cope with global engagement.

Crossing the threshold into the third decade of the twenty-first century, the COVID-19 global pandemic has shown that micro-globalization powered by communication technologies is inevitable and profound on our daily agendas. More forms of virtual global connections ranging from online courses to video consultancy change how we give meaning to our lives and how we build relationships. COVID was a frustrating time for us, and many of us hit a wall in a time of uncertainty. Most people embraced online communities where a bunch of people have become good friends, yet never met in person. The virtual people-based micro-globalization is a myth to understanding virtual ties.

The new generation is not a homogeneous one. The inequalities based on the rural-urban division and social class have led to the unequal development of China's new generation. The rural-to-urban young generation are the majority that contradicts the term "the new generation"; the urbanites have those new generational features that distinguish from the older generations. But they are still ambivalent about the generational gap and a set of rigid Chinese rules & values. They sometimes have to be obedient.

The Chinese will still be Chinese. Probably, tradition is a barrier to Westernization in Chinese modernization. And identity politics is not nurtured in "modernization with Chinese characteristics." For one thing, political economy navigates modernization throughout the world, and Chinese modernization is rooted in paternalism – the state prefers to manage liberty with intervention since Confucian times, and parenting is authoritarian which puts an accent on deference.[37] For another, the degree of openness to Westernization in Chinese modernization is unbalanced to the Chinese people in coastal cities and inland cities – the people in Shanghai, Guangzhou, and Shenzhen are closer to more Western resources, whereas the people in inland Southwest China's Sichuan, Yunnan, and Guizhou accept fewer Western contacts. The majorities and the minorities everywhere are the issues surrounding power relations for modernization as we shall discuss in Chapter 5. The third decade of the twenty-first century is sweeping through every single day, hopefully, people-oriented micro-globalization will shift identities beyond identities for the better in the third decade.

Notes

1 Erikson, Erik. "Theory of Identity Development." *E. Erikson, Identity and the Life Cycle. International Universities Press. Obtenido de http://childdevpsychology.yolasite.com/resources/theory%20of%20ident ity%20erikson.pdf*, 1959.
2 Bernstein, Mary. "Identity Politics." *Annual Review of Sociology*, vol. 31, 2005, pp. 47–74, JSTOR, http://www.jstor.org/stable/29737711.
3 Furedi, Frank. "The Hidden History of Identity Politics." *Spiked The Hidden History of Identity Politics Comments*, Spiked, 13 Oct. 2021, www.spiked-online.com/2017/12/01/the-hidden-history-of-identity-politics/.
4 Fukuyama, Francis. *Identity: Contemporary Identity Politics and the Struggle for Recognition.* Profile Books, 2018.
5 Fukuyama, Francis. *The End of History and the Last Man.* 1st Free Press trade pbk. ed., Free Press, 2006.
6 Ricoeur, Paul, and David Pellauer. *The Course of Recognition.* Harvard University Press, 2005. *JSTOR*, doi:10.2307/j.ctv1dv0tv0. Accessed 16 Apr. 2024.
7 Taylor, Charles. "The Politics of Recognition." *Campus Wars.* Routledge, 2021. 249–63. Also see De Wit, Theo WA.
8 Monnet, Catherine. *Recognition the Key to Identity.* iUniverse, 2015.
9 Fukuyama, Francis. *The End of History and the Last Man.* 1st Free Press trade pbk. ed., Free Press, 2006, pp. 181–91.
10 Marx, Karl. *The Poverty of Philosophy.* Prometheus Books, 1995, p. 121.
11 Eric Louw, P. "The Pax Americana and Development." *Handbook of Communication for Development and Social Change*, edited by Jan Servaes, Springer Singapore, 2020, pp. 167–92. doi:10.1007/978-981-15-2014-3_35.
12 Rostow, W. W. *The Stages of Economic Growth.* 3rd ed., Cambridge University Press, 1991.
13 Lipset, Seymour Martin. "Some Social Requisites of Democracy: Economic Development and Political Legitimacy." *The American Political Science Review*, vol. 53, no. 1, 1959, pp. 69–105. *JSTOR*, doi:10.2307/1951731.
14 Lerner, Daniel. "The Passing of Traditional Society: Modernizing the Middle East." 1958, pp. 52–9.
15 See Eric (2020), pp. 182–90.
16 Rostow, W. W. *The Stages of Economic Growth.* 3rd ed., Cambridge University Press, p. 8, 1991.
17 Jin, Keyu. *The New China Playbook: Beyond Socialism and Capitalism.* Swift Press, 2023, p. 61.
18 Jin, Keyu. *The New China Playbook: Beyond Socialism and Capitalism.* Swift Press, 2023, pp. 59–60.

Also see Choukhmane, Taha et al. "The One-Child Policy and Household Saving." *Journal of the European Economic Association*, vol. 21, no. 3, 2023, pp. 987–1032, doi:10.1093/jeea/jvad001.

19 OECD Data. Household Savings. I selected the data on China's household savings rate of household disposable income in comparison with the four Western countries that Chinese students mostly choose to study: Australia, the United Kingdom, the United States, and Canada. The net household saving rate represents the total amount of net saving as a percentage of net household disposable income. It thus shows how much households are saving out of current income and also how much income they have added to their net wealth. All OECD countries compile their data according to the 2008 System of National Accounts (SNA). https://data.oecd.org/hha/household-savings.htm.
20 "China: Number of Students That Study Abroad." *Statista*, 11 July 2023, www.statista.com/statistics/227240/number-of-chinese-students-that-study-abroad/. Accessed 18 Oct. 2023. The number of Chinese students going abroad for study

kept increasing until 2019. That year, around 703,500 Chinese students left China to pursue overseas studies. The number increased by 6.25 percent compared to the previous year and made China the largest country of origin for international students in the world. According to estimates, numbers have roughly halved in 2020 due to the coronavirus pandemic.

21 I selected the figures of the four Western countries that Chinese students mostly choose to study: Australia, the United Kingdom, the United States, and Canada. And these four Western countries heavily rely on Chinese students. See Tao, (2021), p. 292; ApplyBoard (2022); Stacey, (2022); International Education Canada (2020).

22 Jin, Ruining and Xiao Wang. "'Somewhere I Belong?' A Study on Transnational Identity Shifts Caused by 'Double Stigmatization' among Chinese International Student Returnees During Covid-19 through the Lens of Mindsponge Mechanism." *Frontiers in Psychology*, vol. 13, 2022, pp. 1018843–43, doi:10.3389/fpsyg.2022.1018843.

23 Qi, Grace Yue. "The Importance of English in Primary School Education in China: Perceptions of Students." *Multilingual Education*, vol. 6, no. 1, 2016, pp. 1–18, doi:10.1186/s13616-016-0026-0.

24 Li, Zhenyu. "English Education in China: An Evolutionary Perspective." *People's Daily Online*, 27 Apr. 2020, en.people.cn/n3/2020/0427/c90000-9684652.html.

25 Cheng, An and Qiuying Wang. *Perspectives on Teaching and Learning English Literacy in China*. Springer Netherlands, 2012, pp. 19–33.

26 Li, Chunling. "Children of the Reform and Opening-Up: China's New Generation and New Era of Development." *The Journal of Chinese Sociology*, vol. 7, no. 1, 2020, p. 18, doi:10.1186/s40711-020-00130-x.

27 Freire, Paulo. *Education for Critical Consciousness*. First edition ed., Zed Books, 2021.

28 Dychtwald, Zak. *Young China: How the Restless Generation Will Change Their Country and the World*. St. Martin's Press, 2018.

29 Friedman, Thomas L. *The World Is Flat: A Brief History of the Globalized World in the Twenty-First Century*. Allen Lane, 2005.

30 "A Brief History of Globalization." *World Economic Forum*, www.weforum.org/agenda/2019/01/how-globalization-4-0-fits-into-the-history-of-globalization/. Accessed 18 Oct. 2023.

31 Sun, Jiaming. "Micro Globalization: Methodological Consideration." *International Journal of Arts, Humanities & Social Science,* vol. 02, no. 9, 2021, p. 27. https://ijahss.net/assets/files/1631390986.pdf.

32 Sun, Jiaming. "Micro Globalization: Methodological Consideration." *International Journal of Arts, Humanities & Social Science,* vol. 02, no. 9, 2021, p. 27. https://ijahss.net/assets/files/1631390986.pdf.

33 Li, Chunling. "Children of the Reform and Opening-Up: China's New Generation and New Era of Development." *The Journal of Chinese Sociology*, vol. 7, no. 1, 2020, p. 18, doi:10.1186/s40711-020-00130-x.

34 Dichter, Alex et al. "Chinese Tourists: Dispelling the Myths." *An in-depth look at China's outbound tourist market*, vol. 32, 2018, p. 4. https://www.sedeenchina.com/wp-content/uploads/2018/12/Chinese-Outbound-Tourist-Market-Report.pdf.

35 Katzarska-Miller, Iva and Stephen Reysen. "Globalized Identities." Springer International Publishing AG, 2022, pp. 19–51.

36 Sun, Jiaming. "Micro Globalization: Methodological Consideration." *International Journal of Arts, Humanities & Social Science,* vol. 02, no. 9, 2021, p. 27. https://ijahss.net/assets/files/1631390986.pdf.

37 Jin, Keyu. *The New China Playbook: Beyond Socialism and Capitalism*. Swift Press, 2023, pp.12–3.

2 The Power of Identity

Modernization theory overlooks the mutual development between social connections and technological progress. Over the decades of modernization by leaps and bounds, communication technologies have introduced a multiplicity of behavioral change patterns and a culture of real virtuality. At the time of writing this book (in August 2023), hybrid working mode has become a new normal everywhere. ChatGPT has been unveiled to prompt conversational functions by Open AI for humans to make daily life more productive, which is available for a broad variety of scenarios. Identity lives in a confusing change as it is. The search for identity is also as powerful as techno-economic change around the meaning of our network society according to the Spanish sociologist Manuel Castells who highlighted it in *The Rise of the Network Society*.[1] Despite identity shifts, going beyond identities would not be possible without understanding the power of identity.

The power of identity lies in its ability to foster individuals' actions and relationships, as well as influence the operation of a society at large. From time to time, the power of identity is a conflictive process which profoundly modifies the self and the network society, but not always; it is more an intertwined process between the self and the network society.[2] The pure modernization theory does not touch upon the way of networking practices within the scope of economic growth, technological change, and social integration. In connection with Westernization, networks flow out of weak ties (a type of Western social networking). For "modernization with Chinese characteristics," networks occur deliberately in the manner of guanxi (a type of Chinese social networking). Needless to say, a globalized society is the network society which moves beyond identities for relationships.

Modernization is an evolution of social changes that gauges the power of identity. This chapter takes account of guanxi (a type of Chinese social networking) and weak ties (a type of Western social networking) within the function of network society. Afterward, it sets out to review the power of identity and helps each of us crack the code of identity terms. Hence, I will be referring to one of the Manuel Castells' thought-provoking trilogies entitled

DOI: 10.4324/9781003528180-3

The Power of Identity and using my observations reaching beyond identities from the micro realities within modernization paradigm.

Moving beyond Identities in the Network Society

What is the network society? Although cultural and institutional diversities penetrate all human activities, the network society is similar to the industrial society of the Industrial Age, marking a kind of social structure of our current Information Age. It was prophetic that the networked social structure of the Information Age would be instrumental to reorganizing economic innovation and the meaning of identity elaborated by Manuel Castells in 1996.[3] Manuel Castells is a visionary scholar who has produced a marvelous pile of work vis-à-vis communication, globalization, network society, social movements, and identity. My views about the power of identity in this chapter builds on Castells' insights in *The Power of Identity*, which has, to some extent, molded my own perception of beyond identities in the network society.

All societies are the network society; however, not all the networks are founded on capitalism. The network society has morphed into relationships in the core of human inclusion and exclusion. This directs us to fit guanxi (a way of Chinese social networking) and weak ties (a way of Western social networking). Through the combined transformation of communication technologies and globalization, the network society changes the social contract beyond socialism and capitalism without identity boundaries. Here is a brief account of guanxi and weak ties beyond identities.

Maintaining guanxi is not a far cry from weak ties. They both refer to connections. Then what is the subtle difference? The modern Chinese people have emphasized ties in every aspect of their daily life. Guanxi is a too cultural conceptual phenomenon of Chinese modernization that dates back to kinship networks grounded in Confucian principles – transferred from "five relationships" between ruler and subject, father and son, elder brother and younger brother, husband and wife, as well as between friends. The strength of guanxi ties is frequently a practical mechanism of social exchanges and favor-seeking through "backdoor channels" characterized by sending gifts.[4]

In the context of the decentralized mayor economy of "modernization with Chinese characteristics," guanxi as a social capital continues thriving in the form of social eating, red envelopes, festive greetings, or banquets. These guanxi practices bind the Chinese people to their network society and engage Western investors to do business with the Chinese market. Often on the micro side, if a junior prefers to go to a top school or wants to find a job, good guanxi-connections mobilized by senior kinships with their relatives and acquaintances (shu ren) would be rather helpful. Therefore, strong ties aptly stand for guanxi to understand Chinese modernization, and it never disappears for the Chinese. The Chinese idiom "courtesy suggests reciprocity (礼尚往来 li shang wang lai)" in Confucianism offers the timeless advice to build mutual relationship by giving gifts in the context of favor exchanges for the Chinese. Recent contact trends with the West do not make guanxi lose its importance. Instead, from my own experience with the new generation of Chinese born in the late 1990s or later, guanxi transitions to sort of weak ties behaviors such as coffee catchups, membership events, and community initiatives.

Likewise, weak ties overlap guanxi practices in some ways. However, weak ties are not cultural things in Westernization. Weak ties are more socially valued in the Western network society. The weak ties theory was introduced by the American sociologist Mark Granovetter in the 1973's paper "The Strength of Weak Ties" in which an accent on weak ties is more valuable for a new opportunity network that is composed of strangers or acquaintances with mutual connections who are more likely to be novel information sources for people to pursue opportunities. In contrast, strong ties are usually composed of people who share a host of same interests and experiences, which are less likely to promote diverse sources.[5]

The empirical real-life stark difference between guanxi and weak ties is casual mentorship experience. Having had both educational experiences in China and the West, my nuanced perspective is – a mentoring network is of little social emphasis in the Chinese network society throughout a student's study life although guanxi is a part of the Chinese culture. In the West, a mentoring network is a meaningful process for a student's growth. A casual mentor with whom a student spends time sharing ideas and challenges sometimes can put in a good word for potential opportunities and guide professional lives. And in every semester, schools and universities usually roll out a variety of mentorship programs in partnership with enterprises in the character of coffee chats, brunch meetups, professional events for employment opportunities, marketing promotions, business engagement, etc.

The present breakthrough in communication technologies embeds us in the network society excluding identity boundaries of cultural and national borders. Such a relational network cultivates guanxi and weak ties via algorithm, affecting a social contract governed by technological changes in addition to economic growth. Today TikTok launched by Confucian China influences billions of users around the world based on weak ties as a result of information sharing and short video marketing. Relevant research reveals that TikTok offers a mode of algorithmizing networked self rather than one's social connections. TikTok evades purposeful identity communities and social networks,[6] so much so that it transcends identities and engenders algorithmized self in the network society.

Another implication for moving beyond identities in the network society is the application of the world's largest professional network LinkedIn also associated with algorithm. Relationships on LinkedIn consist of a core set of strangers that experts commonly call weak ties. Using data from 20 million LinkedIn profiles suggested by "People You May Know" algorithm, the study in 2022 co-authored by LinkedIn and MIT researchers demonstrates that weak ties on average are more useful than strong ties to add new job-hunting value, particularly for more digital industries in the context of such digital identities of the global economy.[7]

Insomuch as the massive convenience of the fast modern and global networks attest to our micro realities that guanxi behavior and weak ties speak volumes of a commonality of humankind as social beings. Either way, guanxi and weak ties are affiliated to social penetration theory – the onion metaphor we peel back each other's layers through an exchange of information under the "law of reciprocity."[8] More unconventionally, the art of romantic love has catalyzed economic growth via in-app purchases on dating apps and networking sites for perfect match. The State of Mobile 2023 report from the data analytics platform Data.ai shows that global consumer spending in dating apps hit 5.9 billion US dollars in 2022. That is a 12 percent year-on-year increase. And Confucian China's consumer spending in dating apps exceeded 20 million US dollars as of the end of 2022.[9]

Moving beyond identities in the network society is too amazing to rely on the pure modernization theory. All this relates to the necessity of modern humans – mutual relationships.

Social Movements and Identity

The power of identity in the network society jointly pushes modernization and globalization. Identity influences identity politics in the modern Western world; good or bad, it has an impact on society by and large. As for social movements, identity is envisioned as the embryo to facilitate collective actions. For Manuel Castells, identities are constructed with three types that make sense of the network society regarding social movements. And there are both progressive movements and regressive movements in accordance with identities. In Chapter 1, we learned that identity terms could promote each community's agenda along with modern identities, while this section covers the three types of identities distinguished by Manuel Castells: *legitimizing identity*, *resistance identity*, and *project identity* in order to crack the code of the identity terms.

Legitimizing identity simply fits with the validity of national identity dominated by a state.[10] Although Castells attributed a diminishing national identity to globalization, Chapter 1 has suggested that globalization no doubt creates a slew of opportunities for individuals to be better than traditional as a result of international trade, technological breakthroughs, and cross-cultural exchanges. Micro-globalization makes identities more diversified. Yet, legitimizing identity is not fading away just because of the flow of globalization, and this identity is very fundamental to participating in micro-globalization. At the micro level, national identity is the essence of identification to travel, employment, and residency in spite of being a global consumer. If you are keen on carving out a career abroad, at least you must hold a local legal *legitimizing identity* document for full unrestricted rights, say, a working visa. If you check in at the airport or a hotel, you need to prove your *legitimizing identity* such as a passport issued by the political institution. If you migrate to another country, you should obtain a permanent residency identity granted by the government. It is *legitimizing identity* that rationalizes the social actors of authorities. Putting aside different ideologies, every nation-state is trying to strengthen *legitimizing identity* by devising a variety of social movements together with migration programs, vaccination campaigns, and national festivals.

In the context of *resistance identity*, people build their communities different from the identities established by institutions. *Resistance identity* is usually generated on the basis of rejection and exclusion, whether economic, social, or cultural. As such, the emergence of social movements in reference to identity politics has identities formed in terms of religion, race, sex, and ethnicity.[11] The social movements of resistance identity may not only empower the actors but also trigger division among various groups. There are diverging demands in every society. After all, we are human beings regardless of identities. For Indigenous communities throughout the world, the battles are indeed resistance identities to reassert their cultures and ancestral land against modern humans within the modernization paradigm.

A *project identity* can be formed when a *resistance identity* becomes strong enough for people to articulate a vision and a mission.[12] This means humans will build a new identity to redefine their position in society. By introducing new sets of values, this is the most powerful aspect of the power of identity in running every society. This is the case for social movements themed the environmental movement to work toward zero emissions by 2050 or the Sustainable Development Goals. Sometimes, *project identity* utterly changes conventional values and *legitimizing identity* to institutionalize it.

Having reviewed *the Power of Identity* by Manuel Castells and plunged into the modern world myself, it is true that identity per se does not induce demands. The power of identity is a process that cannot be separable from experiences, be it *legitimizing identity*, *resistance identity*, or *project identity*. Now, let's make sense of our world.

Making Sense of Our World

The importance of a passport secures a person traveling abroad to prove identity. It grants the bearer safe passage and legitimate protection in a foreign land. In this sense, a passport is considered a symbolic legitimacy asset to achieve an identity that is instrumentalized as a means of identity. The talk then goes as follows: I am Chinese, you are Singaporean, he is American, she is Canadian, and so on. People identify themselves with the titular documents recognized by a state. Unlike the power of identity, the power of a passport is a reflection of a state's economy that serves as a source of visa exemption with specific countries besides diplomatic factors.

Contemporary study on identity in sports has revealed that identity is an evolving cultural construction that informs narrative research.[13] When it comes to sports, there is no alleged West or East because the national anthem of each society ignites the spark for their legitimizing identities, namely, nationalism. We are part of the exciting vibes that we cheer for our own *legitimizing identity* representative of citizenship dominated by a state at the Olympics, FIFA, and World Championship Games. I vividly remember every Chinese was proudly rooting for the Chinese national team and singing the national anthem of People's Republic of China at events of the 2008 Beijing Olympics when Beijing played host to the marvelous international sports engagement back in 2008. Even though the Chinese people watched the 2008 sporting events in front of televisions including me, the pride intensified by *legitimizing identity* has demonstrated a piece of unity that subconsciously motivates each legitimate individual to support the national team.

Fast forward the moments to the 2023 FIFA Women's World Cup hosted by Australia and New Zealand (ANZ), audiences in the two multicultural countries predominantly followed their teams depending on *legitimizing identity* as a nation. I saw this uplifting nationalism in the play-off for the third place between the Australian national team "The Matildas" and the Swedish national team "Blågult." Before kick-off, the ritual of playing national anthems appeared to legitimize each other's national identity as Australian and Swedish. At Southbank Parklands in Brisbane on the outdoor live screen, I watched the audience surrounding me not saying we were the West, but we were Australians, they were Swedish. When the national anthem of Sweden went up, I noticed only Swedish in the stadium stood up and sang the national anthem of Sweden with some waving the Swedish national flags, whereas the Australians around me at Southbank were sitting on the grass and chatting. A second later, when the national anthem of Australia rang out, the Australians in the stadium and at Southbank ended their dialogues, stood up right away, and proudly sang aloud the national anthem of Australia. And vice versa for the Swedish. We never hear West or East in sports, just legitimizing identities beyond identities.

Against the backdrop of the COVID-19 pandemic, legitimizing identities were capable of coping with the contagion. In spite of an interdependent time, measures were centralized by giving up travel borders to trading partners and rolling out vaccination movements for each modernity's solidarity. Australia touted "a stronger, safer, and together Australia" to promote the vaccination rate. New Zealand appealed "Unite against COVID-19" in both the local Maori language and the English language on social media sites with the purpose of a shared legitimizing identity as a nation. China took an authoritative "zero tolerance" COVID strategy to keep the virus at bay and glorify the great Chinese history. America billed every phase as American Exceptionalism to demonstrate "America is great again." No matter what legitimizing identity you smile on, the legitimacy of a legitimizing identity has power.

Identities are powerful against legitimizing identities, and resistance identities build interests, values, and actions around experiences that choose to defend their autonomy and desires. Resistance identities oppose traditional values and negotiate legitimizing identities. There is no denying that patriarchalism is alive and well around the world, and this tradition remains the cornerstone of institutions in every society. However, the identities of gays and lesbians, the weakening of marital relations by divorce, and the fostering of future generations without marriage call into question the patriarchal way of life, which is increasing the likelihood of single parenthood and stepfamilies. The recognition of these anti-patriarchal movements is an example of what an identity resists and projects.

Both developed and developing societies have undergone this rising trend since 1960s. A study published by Pew Research Center in 2019 (See Figure 2.1) shows that the United States has led the highest rate of single-parent households in the world, with a quarter of American children under 18 years living in single-parenthood families. The share of neighboring Canada is around 15 percent. In populous societies like China and India, the percentages of children under the age of 18 living in single-parent families account for 3 percent and 5 percent, respectively.[14] In particular, such single

Almost a quarter of U.S. children live in single-parent homes, more than in any other country

% of children under age 18 in single-parent households

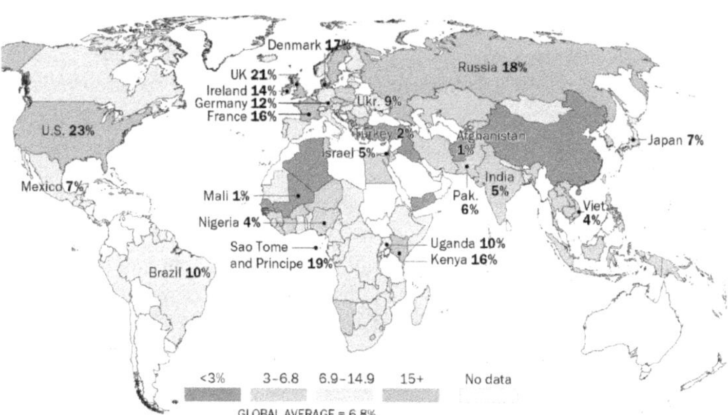

Note: Single-parent households include one adult and at least one biological, step or foster child under 18. Adult children may be present, but no other relatives or non-relatives.
Source: Pew Research Center analysis of 2010-2018 census and survey data. See methodology for details.
"Religion and Living Arrangements Around the World"

PEW RESEARCH CENTER

Figure 2.1 Percentage of children under age 18 in single-parent households.

Source: Reprinted with the permission of Pew Research Center.[14]

parenthood triggers a rising proportion of female-headed households (both unmarried women with children and single moms after divorce). Globally, the median percentage of households headed by women from 2010 to 2019 was 28 percent. Across regions, it varied from 36 percent in Latin America & Caribbean to 23 percent in East Asia and the Pacific.[15]

These female-headed households undermine our perceptions of patriarchal dominance institutionally, psychologically, and culturally as Manuel Castells stated. Under the condition of female-headed households, modernization finds its own new way in opposition to patriarchy and has reconstructed resistance identities over family for an egalitarian basis, implying the gender stereotype on the traditional patriarchal family strips away.

On the other hand, technological change in reproduction opens up possibilities of cultivating future generations by means of vitro fertilization, sperm banks, surrogate mothers, and genetically engineered babies. Both female-headed families, women and sexual identity movements use technology to enhance reproductive rights, redefining what it means to be a parent and a full human being.[16] In this day and age, we are seeing the relationship between biology and socialization reverse legitimizing identities in every society for being a woman, a mother, and a wife. This is contradictory; so, Castells alerted that those reproductive technologies posed a threat to our societies based on morality and legitimacy.

In the re-interpretation of the code of identity politics by Manuel Castells, "At the moment when humankind reaches the technological frontier of social control over the biological reproduction of the species, a fundamental battle is being fought between bodies as autonomous identities and bodies as social artifacts. This is why identity politics starts with our bodies."[17] At the dawn of the twenty-first century in the book *The Great Disruption: Human Nature and the Reconstitution of Social Order*, Francis Fukuyama brilliantly observed that the disruption of social order by the progress of technology and family breakdown would seek out new ones by means of human reason to create moral rules and negotiate our needs and passions.[18] Being a female myself, I am delighted to live in a modern era of options for fertility powered by technologies. At the same time, I am more concerned about morality and the aftershock of this resistance identity to future generations around the world.

A decade after the pronouncement of "the end of history," Francis Fukuyama's *Our Posthuman Future: Consequences of the Biotechnology Revolution* argues that our future humanity will be altered beyond recognition as a consequence of biotechnology advances even if technology should be legitimately regulated.[19] This kind of view misses the point of resistance in humanity to be modern dignity and safety, and the power of being as resistance identities as we shall discuss later. There is supply and demand in the profitable biotech industry, and such resistance identity against the fundamental structure of any society – patriarchalism – will be a trial for the legitimatizing identities within modernization paradigm.

We have welcomed the diffusion of global flows of economy and information. The outcome of identity shifts might generate project identities that aim at transforming a society. This is why identities are so important as Manuel Castells highlighted. These new identities inspire people to legitimize another identity. We are feeling that extreme weather events have enormously affected the everyday mood around us, flooding being a case in point. The 2022 Queensland and New South Wales floods in Australia had endured more than a year's worth of rainfall from late February to early April that caused the devastation of thousands of homes.[20] The scale of climate change is disastrous in northern hemisphere, too. Severe torrential rains hit many parts of China in the aftermath of Typhoon Doksuri in August 2023, forcing millions of people to evacuate with the swallow of infrastructures and districts. It also lashed the Philippines, Japan, and India with waterlogged large swath of suburbs.[21] During the same period, heatwave has shown no sign of abating, and residents across the globe continue to grapple with scorching temperatures and wildfires, whether you are in Greece, Spain, Italy, France, America, Japan, or China.[22] These ferocious micro realities project an identity to defend one's environment and well-being with nature as humankind. As a result, people project a new identity for the sustainable development agenda and manage to legitimize it by hosting sustainable weeks, launching sustainable programs, and setting zero emissions by 2050 in most societies at present.

Studies suggest that the everyday climate is closely related to people who champion climate friendly value – this is an expression of a person's self through the intrinsic internalization of "me as an environmentalist" alongside climate-friendly manners and lifestyles. Environmental self-identity is a generational shift in identity and a global consciousness for one planet to tackle climate change.[23] This is a "global identity," which transcends identities in the form of environmental movements and convenes the UN's annual Climate Change Conference.

Having said that, the communes of each identity preserve their spaces, their places, their values to organize activities and participate in interactions. In this sense, if identities per se are prioritized, they cannot be transcended. Next, we are about to read multiculturalism and migration in Chapter 3.

Notes

1 Castells, Manuel. *The Rise of the Network Society.* vol. 12, John Wiley & Sons, Incorporated, 2009, p. 4.

2 Castells, Manuel. *The Rise of the Network Society.* vol. 12, John Wiley & Sons, Incorporated, 2009, p. 3.

3 Castells, Manuel. "The Network Society Revisited." *The American Behavioral Scientist (Beverly Hills)*, vol. 67, no. 7, 2023, pp. 940–46, doi:10.1177/00027642221092803.

4 Krausse, Reuss-Markus. *Guanxi as a Model of Social Integration.* Humanities Online, 2010.

5 Granovetter, Mark S. "The Strength of Weak Ties." *American Journal of Sociology*, vol. 78, no. 6, 1973, pp. 1360–80.

6 Bhandari, Aparajita, and Sara Bimo. “Why’s Everyone on TikTok Now? The Algorithmized Self and the Future of Self-making on Social Media.” *Social Media + Society*, vol. 8, no. 1, 2022, p. 20563051221086241.

7 Rajkumar, Karthik, et al. “A Causal Test of the Strength of Weak Ties.” *Science*, vol. 377, no. 6612, 2022, pp. 1304–10.

8 Carpenter, Amanda, and Kathryn Greene. “Social Penetration Theory.” *The International Encyclopedia of Interpersonal Communication*, edited by C.R. Berger, M.E. Roloff, S.R. Wilson, J.P. Dillard, J. Caughlin and D. Solomon, 2015, pp. 1–4.

9 “Data.Ai: State of Mobile 2023: En by Localization / Final.” *Infogram*, 2023, dataai.infogram.com/1pv12merg7e3e7axedy3mmpvvjirpge6z7x?mkt_tok=MDcxLVFFRC0yODQAAAGQfXN3KhRpyRQuUewcnuP604RFX37ROWsBPZXO9R789Ouyd_2v5Fnkolcjkdp WeC6_a0d7QkKGEHuAwbxg2X51ZK2KyVQuZo07O4iOHT9s5LDUx7pt. Accessed 06 Jan. 2024.

10 Castells Manuel. *The Power of Identity Volume II.* 2nd, with a new preface ed., Wiley-Blackwell, 2010, pp. 7–8.

11 Castells Manuel. *The Power of Identity Volume II.* 2nd, with a new preface ed., Wiley-Blackwell, 2010, pp. 7–8.

12 Castells Manuel. *The Power of Identity Volume II.* 2nd, with a new preface ed., Wiley-Blackwell, 2010, pp. 7–8.

13 Eubank, Martin et al. “New Approaches to Identity in Sport.” *Journal of Sport Psychology in Action*, vol. 11, no. 4, 2020, pp. 215–18, doi:10.1080/21520704.2020.1835134.

14 Kramer, Stephanie. “U.S. Has World’s Highest Rate of Children Living in Single-Parent Households.” *Pew Research Center*, 12 Dec. 2019, www.pewresearch.org/short-reads/2019/12/12/u-s-children-more-likely-than-children-in-other-countries-to-live-with-just-one-parent/. Accessed 3 Mar. 2024.

15 Saad, Ghada E., et al. “Paving the Way to Understanding Female-headed Households: Variation in Household Composition across 103 Low- and Middle-income Countries.” *Journal of Global Health* 12, 2022, p. 5.

16 Castells Manuel. *The Power of Identity Volume II.* 2nd, with a new preface ed., Wiley-Blackwell, 2010, pp. 423–425.

17 Castells Manuel. *The Power of Identity Volume II.* 2nd, with a new preface ed., Wiley-Blackwell, 2010, p. 424.

18 Fukuyama, Francis. *The Great Disruption: Human Nature and the Reconstitution of Social Order.* Touchstone, 2000.

19 Fukuyama, Francis. *Our Posthuman Future: Consequences of the Biotechnology Revolution.* Farrar, Straus and Giroux, 2003.

20 “One Year on from the 2022 QLD and NSW Floods: National Emergency Management Agency.” *2022 QLD and NSW Floods | National Emergency Management Agency*, 24 Feb. 2023, nema.gov.au/2022-QLD-and-NSW-floods.

21 “Typhoon Doksuri: Alarming Pictures Show Floods in China, Philippines.” *BBC News*, BBC, 5 Aug. 2023, www.bbc.com/news/in-pictures-66400905. Accessed 3 Mar. 2024.

22 “Heatwaves Set More Records across Europe, Asia and US.” *Weather News | Al Jazeera*, 19 July 2023, www.aljazeera.com/news/2023/7/19/heatwaves-set-more-records-across-europe-asia-and-usa. Accessed 3 Mar. 2024.

23 Masson, Torsten and Immo Fritsche. “Adherence to Climate Change-Related Ingroup Norms: Do Dimensions of Group Identification Matter?” *European Journal of Social Psychology*, vol. 44, no. 5, 2014, pp. 455–65, doi:10.1002/ejsp.2036. See Vesely, Stepan et al. Also see Chen, Wei-Ting, and Ming-Huei Hsieh, and Seary, Kate.

3 Multiculturalism and Migration

Modernization means constant change and disruption, and the opening up of choices that did not exist before. It is mobile, fluid, and complex. This fluidity is by and large a good thing: over generations, millions of people have been fleeing villages and traditional societies that do not offer them choices, in favor of ones that do... The authentic identities they are seeking are ones that bind them to other people.[1]

(Francis Fukuyama, Identity: Contemporary Identity Politics and the Struggle for Recognition, p. 164)

Modernization cannot be figured out without migration. Migration is one of the most spectacular and controversial phenomena in every economy past, present, and future. We are the descendants of migrants, not to mention myself. I framed modernizing identities for the new generation of Chinese in Chapter 1, and the migration was my footprint that has shaped my flow of thought in this chapter to burrow into multiculturalism and migration. With my lived experiences in China, multicultural Australia, and traveling, this chapter attempts to look beyond identities through an exploration of internal migration in China, international migration, and multiculturalism in Australia.

Migration is going on. The common sense is that the decision to migrate is about becoming an identity, and the migration policies of each nation play an instrumental role in coordinating the movement and legitimizing identities. At times, the question "Where are you from" gives rise to self-hesitation and an abandonment of other identities. For everyone on all sides of migration, I will fit research and micro realities into this magnificent movement within modernization paradigm.

We Are Migrants

My mother was born and brought up in a village called Zhang Jiaqiao in Sichuan Province of Southwest China, affiliated with my birthplace Qiuxi Town. She has told me about her struggle from tradition to modernity hundreds of

DOI: 10.4324/9781003528180-4

times, and the saving process of my family to evolve into a middle-class. My grandparents typically favored boys over girls driven by the long-traditional Chinese gender preference. They lived in a thatched cottage and raised three daughters and a son. Pit latrines used to be the defining feature of their life in rural Southwest China, dirty and smelly, following flies in an endless stream. At that time in the late 1980s and the early 1990s, my mother and the big aunt went into society at an average young age of 20 to put through their family and worked hard in town. The older generation of my family was determined to get rid of backwardness in the village, so they moved away from the infertile and immobile societies in rural Southwest China. The magnet of urban life has offered mesmerizing economic opportunities and better life quality for its offspring. Years afterward, my modern journey started from the late 1990s that I have alluded to in Chapter 1.

By definition, the United Nations' migration agency, International Organization for Migration (IOM), states that a migrant is any person who moves within a country or across an international border away from one's habitual residence irrespective of a person's legal status, categories of the movement, motivations for the movement, or length of the stay.[2]

"Modernization with Chinese characteristics" is uniquely managed by political centralization paired with economic decentralization of the mayor economy and so is its migration or also floating population. The bulk of Chinese internal migration operates under heavy state intervention that not only achieves modern China's spectacular economy but also distributes social benefits across rural and urban areas. Chinese internal migration has never receded. The permanent household registration (hukou) system is the epitome of a green card that encourages better modern desires of the Chinese people. Hukou system has stimulated rural-urban migration over the past four decades in modern China. Throughout the 1980s until the mid-1990s, hukou system strictly excluded rural migrants from the equal social benefits as urban residents, including education, employment, pensions, and subsidized housing. Notwithstanding, the massive influx of rural migrants chose to land a place in cities along with China's economic boom.[3] These rural migrants were young and poorly educated like the older generation of my family, yet they put their noses to the grindstone across construction, manufacturing, and social services industries to create a brighter future for their children and grandchildren.

As the macro social reforms have gradually relaxed hukou system since 2000, migration in China allows greater mobility and rural migrants to settle down. However, the social progress of Chinese internal migration in part lags behind economic growth – a high Chinese value in hierarchy since Confucian times has positioned discrimination by urban hukou holders against rural hukou holders. Meanwhile, hukou system largely denies the children of rural migrants to obtain public education and healthcare in cities, so many migrants without urban hukou permanent residency leave their children behind with relatives or grandparents and send back financial remittances.[4] According to the People's Republic of China's Seventh National Population Census in 2020, the population of the rural-urban migrants' group has reached up to some 376 million, which is nearly 70 percent greater than that in 2010 within modernization paradigm.[5]

No doubt that the expansion of the Chinese decentralized economy thrives with Chinese internal migration. During my childhood, I liked watching the popular TV comedy-drama "The Bang-bang Army in Mount Chongqing City" (*Shan Cheng Bang-bang Jun*), which was dedicated to the bang-bang army in Chongqing City of Southwest China known as itinerant porters who were one of the key builders of Chinese economic modernization. These migrants hailed from rural villages around Chongqing to make a living by using their stamina to carry loads. Bang-bang porters clutching poles and bundles of rope earned each penny with sweat, and it was a tough profession with pretty low pay equivalent to at most 1 US dollar per hauling. At their peak, the number of bang-bang porters hit as many as 300,000 in the 1990s in the city.[6] Even so, the job is vanishing as modern transportation has cut the demand for the back-breaking hauling work and fast couriers in e-commerce are more promising. The aging of bang-bang porters is also in miniature of a choice in modernity that younger, better-educated migrants often reject the poorly paid and harsh role.[7] To some degree, human beings always long for a better life.

With a population of over 1.4 billion, China observes the largest annual human migration on earth – Chun Yun known as Chinese Lunar New Year or Spring Festival. Every year hundreds of millions of Chinese people migrate in and out of their hometowns within a period of 40 days. Holidays in modern China are mainly governed by lunisolar calendar regulating lunar months and solar years. For the Chinese people, the identity binding them to others is reunion of quality time that is analogous to Christmas in Western modernization. Although Western cultures have an influence on the new generation of Chinese, tradition in "modernization with Chinese characteristics" has yet stifled the millennia-old Chinese customs such as lighting firecrackers and fortune telling.

The other catchphrase of internal migration in China was about a wave of adventure to *Xia Hai*, "plunging into the sea" of private business. This migration movement emerged when China was entering into market economy in the 1980s. Business opportunities came up and inspired lots of people to start up in coastal cities in Guangdong Province, Fujian Province, Zhejiang Province, Liaoning Province, and Shanghai. Most of these migrants to the coastal cities were employed by government, state-run factories, or institutes, and they quit jobs to open their own businesses.[8] This exodus to get rich has marked a modern mindset for change that outmoded values could not offer humans as immense opportunities as the modern economy.

Nowadays, people are constantly on the move in the buzz and excitement of modern China. The present-day migrants are younger and highly educated toward a new vision equipped with modern communications and exposed to the changing sense of identities with micro-globalization. Research findings show that born into the era of opening up in Chinese modernization, the new generation of more skilled Chinese migrants is motivated to earn more, enjoy more, and consume more.[9] In a word, it has been better than "traditional."

International migration is an additional tendency either yesterday, today, or tomorrow. It is not easy to collect accurate international migration data. For one thing, international migration is unpredictable in motion worldwide; for another, the statistics are often scattered across different organizations. The available World Migration Report 2022 from the United Nations' IOM suggests that international migrants worldwide comprise 3.6 percent of the global population, and the number grew to almost 281 million in 2020. This has been an increasing trend over the past three decades (see Figure 3.1).[10]

Geographically in 2020, Europe and Asia have the most international migrants with an estimated 86.7 million and 85.6 million, respectively, followed by 58.7 million in North America and 25.4 million in Africa. The Latin America and Caribbean region have roughly doubled to 14.8 million international migrants since 2005. In terms of the share of population, the larger portion of international migrants in Oceania overtook other regions, with around 21 percent of international residents making up Oceania's population, including Australia, New Zealand, and Pacific Island nations. Nonetheless, regional groupings in Gulf Cooperation Council countries such as Kuwait, the United Arab Emirates, Saudi Arabia, Qatar, Bahrain, and Oman have more than half international resident populations (see Figure 3.2). Despite the fact that the United States leads more international migrants by a wide margin with around

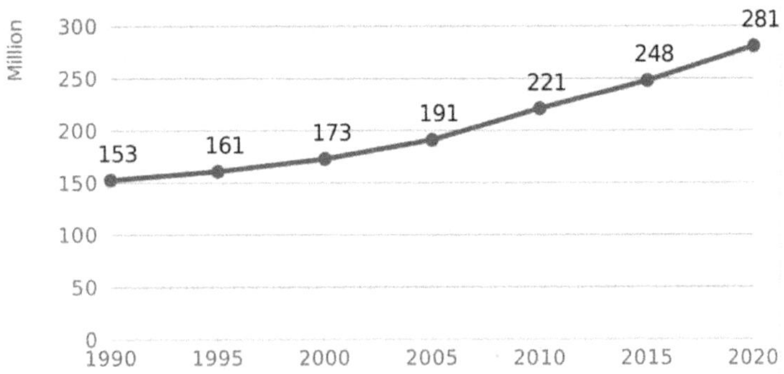

Figure 3.1 Global trend of international migrants (both sexes combined).

Source: From International Migration Stock 2020 by Population Division of the United Nation. Reprinted with the permission of the United Nations. https://www.un.org/development/desa/pd/content/international-migrant-stock.

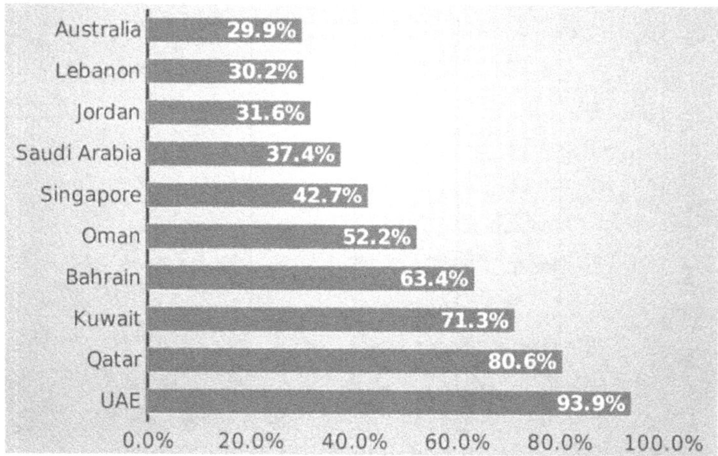

Figure 3.2 Percentage of the country's population that are international migrants in 2020.

Source: Adapted from Pew Research Center with permission. Natarajan, Anusha, et al. "Key Facts about Recent Trends in Global Migration | Pew Research Center." Pew Research Center, 16 Dec. 2022, https://www.pewresearch.org/short-reads/2022/12/16/key-facts.

51 million in 2020 (see Figure 3.3), the countries that have the most international migrants are generally *not* the same countries where international migrants make up the greatest share of the population. Migrants only represent about 15 percent of the US population. By 2020, more than 90 percent of people living in the United Arab Emirates were international migrants.[11]

The motives for international migration are intricate. Economists are usually of the view that a richer elsewhere chiefly motivates people to desperately migrate from low-income societies to high-income societies. In some cases, people move to escape wars or persecution. Environmental factors occasionally force both internal migration and international migration in response to natural disasters or pollution. Apart from that, the final decision to international migration is an individual choice with regard to religion, education, marriage, or personal attitude to lifestyles.[12]

Deep down, migration is proceeding with hyper-connected modernization. Francis Fukuyama put it in the book *Identity: Contemporary Identity Politics and the Struggle for Recognition*, "Modernization means constant change and disruption, and the opening up of choices that did not exist before. It is mobile, fluid, and complex. This fluidity is by and large a good thing: over generations, millions of people have been fleeing villages and traditional societies that do not offer them choices, in favor of ones that do… The authentic identities they are seeking are ones that bind them to other people."[13] Either way, the stories of every migrant are based on their lived experience to define

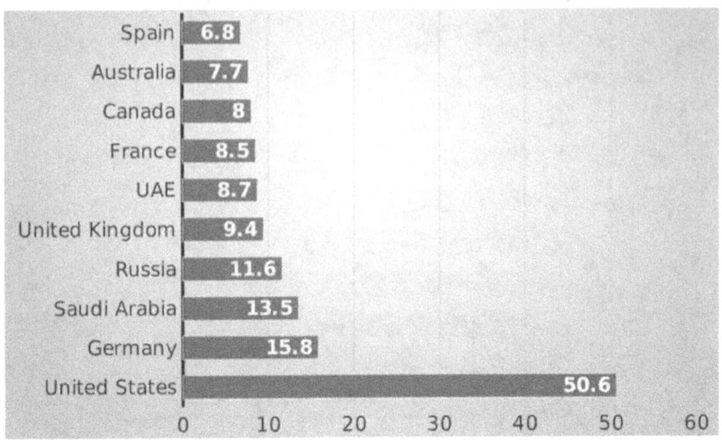

Figure 3.3 The number of international migrants by Country, in millions, 2020.

Source: Adapted from Pew Research Center with permission. Natarajan, Anusha, et al. "Key Facts about Recent Trends in Global Migration | Pew Research Center." Pew Research Center, 16 Dec. 2022, https://www.pewresearch.org/short-reads/2022/12/16/key-facts

an identity. But the essence is that we are human beings beyond identities on the move.

The Consequences of International Migration

Restrictions during the COVID-19 pandemic have put all categories of migration on hold in most societies. As a result, a drop in migration inflows has demographic effects on societies that rely upon migration for population growth and labor force. In Australia, lower overseas migration inflows than outflows in 2020–2021 have brought about the lowest population growth since the Second World War.[14] In Germany, the population did not grow for the first time over the last decade due to a sharp decline in foreign migration inflows throughout the pandemic, and the number of old people aged over 80 continued to increase.[15] In Canada, although immigrants helped to mitigate low fertility rates and aging population with four-fifths of labor force growth from 2016 to 2021, the pandemic-related lockdowns disrupted economic integration of many migrants.[16]

Migration has come to terms with macro policies that catalyze a chain of agents assisting people to relocate here and there. Macro migration policies are adjusted every financial year in host societies by classifying a multiplicity of visa types and updating rules. An array of micro competitions, in some senses, have been brought into being. For example, host societies normally set an annual upper limit of places available for a permanent residency visa, and the migration cap in a number of economies is simultaneously introduced with points-based immigration systems, including the United Kingdom, Australia, Canada, Singapore, Hong Kong, and so on. If you express your interest in immigration, you must be able to score above a threshold number of points in a scoring system. The points-based immigration systems are relevant to such factors as wealth, occupation, age criterion, work experience, language level, educational background, and nominated skill certificates.

At this point, a grueling in-group competition among migrants from original societies is in cycle, which impels immigrants to jockey for an identity of host societies. Agents come to rival comprehensive information to serve potential clients. Business organizations contend with rankings for diversity and inclusion of the best workplace. From my knowledge, some migrants spend hundreds of thousands of dollars to realize an identity of host societies; some devote five years or more to an identity pathway to the first rung of host societies; and some choose a local partner of host societies to become an identity.

Indeed, migration is an inevitable facet of globalization. As economies are on the mend in the post-pandemic era, a new wave of migration has temporarily come back to normality of the pre-pandemic level. Canada sets a target to receive 1.5 million new residents in the period of 2023–2025. Germany and India signed a joint agreement to allow more Indians to work and study in Germany. Australia is on track for the pre-COVID level of 190,000 places in the 2023–2024 Permanent Migration Program. Even those countries that are closed to overseas migration, including Japan and South Korea, are now favoring outsiders as they seek to counteract the impact of aging populations.[17] In response to the balanced economic and social development, migration numbers can be unexpectedly tightened. Therefore, migration policies are flexible any time.

Other than the micro-competition among migrants, agents, and business organizations, the economic and social consequences are equally important in international migration. In his illuminating book *Exodus: Immigration and Multiculturalism in the Twenty-first Century*, the British economist Paul Collier tells us that the nuanced relationship between migrants and the Indigenous population of host societies in the social effects should be put ahead of the economic effects.[18] Migration brings greater diversity which consists of not only numbers but also cultural distance. By referring to mutual regard akin to sympathy, trust, and cooperation, Paul Collier argues that the Indigenous of host societies can fail to recognize migrants as members of a common society, and migrants can unsuccessfully recognize the Indigenous. Macro migration policies permit migrants to preserve their cultures of origin, but the preservation of cultures may not reflect the preservation of identities of the societies of origin. So, the key issue raised by Paul Collier is: do both migrants and the Indigenous of host societies come to see each other as members of a common society?[19] In this respect, I will be relating the question to multicultural Australia in the next section "Be Immersed in Multiculturalism."

Economically speaking, while international migration increases the economic performance and innovation of host societies, the economic consequences can be controversial too. The economic impacts are open-ended questions. Migration fills labor shortages and boosts working-age populations, but is it a virtuous cycle for micro-competition? If large swath of migrants poured into host societies, would it be good or bad for the housing stock and the social services? Migration aggregates the overall gross domestic product (GDP) of host societies; is this situation also clear to per capita GDP growth? Can immigrants offset aging populations confronting both developed societies and developing societies today?[20] With all due respect, I am of the view that understanding these impacts varies from context to context considering the modernization circumstances of different societies, which transcends a spectrum of identities.

As to the societies of origin, the implications of the social and economic consequences for host societies will be likely to be the opposite in the societies of origin.[21] Evidently, remittances from emigrants sent back home have a positive effect on the improvement of household income and quality of life. The data released by the World Bank show that recorded financial remittances of migrants to low- and middle-income societies grew 5 percent to 626 billion US dollars in 2022, helping recipients in home societies cope with their family finance and investment opportunities.[22] Besides, social remittances play a role in building the socio-economic development of home societies when return migrants bring back new ideas and social capital from host societies. Indirectly, identities can be reformed after contacting the languages, cultures, and lifestyles of host societies.[23] This consequence in social remittances comparably fits in modernizing identities for the new generation of Chinese as we have read about the account of Chinese international students' exposure to Western modernization earlier. Whether "brain drain" or "brain gain" for the societies of origin and host societies, my observation is that this matter will be accompanied by the mobile micro-competition in modernity, and it is up to the interactions between macro migration policies and migrants themselves.

Be Immersed in Multiculturalism

Continuous movements make societies colorful, and diversity creates a broad range of innovations coupled with multiculturalism. This is enriched by the global flows of talent, ideas, and capital. The American sitcom television *Fresh Off the Boat* depicts how a Chinese American family in the 1990s has assimilated into the melting pot of American communities whose multiculturalism reflects issues of identity, race, ethnicity, as well as migration. From where I stand, being immersed in multiculturalism within modernization paradigm can be a multifaceted explanation. To this end, I will be sharing my familiarity with multiculturalism in Australia.

Australia was not of the West, and I am not of the West. My eyes look at Australia from the outside in. This lonely land of Indigenous Australians is considered the oldest ceaseless civilization on earth, which dates back to 65,000 years ago. The First Nations People of this land, Aboriginal and Torres Strait Islander peoples representing 3.2 percent of the Australian population, remind me of the far-flung ideologically opposite China where the Chinese people regard Westernization as exotica, while Indigenous Australians call the West the Western people. The early landings in Australia by Dutch and Spanish explorers in the seventeenth century marked names mapping of the Australian mainland and coasts.[24] Captain James Cook planted the British flags on the Australian soil in 1770, as if this was an empty land. As the First Fleet arrived at Botany Bay in New South Wales on January 20, 1788, Australia's national day is steeped in a history of colonialization – what Indigenous people call the invasion and theft of their lands. Gold rushes and immigrants brought prosperity to modern Australia, and the modernization is not separate from British Empire, the Stolen Generations, mass immigration, reconciliation, and apology. Multiculturalism is a central feature of the modern Australian identity as a result of successive waves of migration that support Australia's economic success.

The 2021 Australian Census highlights that more than half of Australian residents were born overseas or have at least one parent born overseas. And over 5.5 million Australians speak at least two languages at home.[25] In the eyes of Stan Grant, the Indigenous Australian of Wiradjuri known as a senior journalist, "born between the ship and the shore, it is the space where I become an Australian even though we are still not sure what being an Australian truly means."[26] For better or worse, the unresolved question of Aussie modernity grapples with a true sovereignty – who truly owns this land?

Without doubt, Australia is a wonderful multicultural society in the world with more than 300 distinctive ancestries. The most ancient surviving folklore of Indigenous Australians lives on in my heart beyond identities. On top of that, exposure to Australia gives me food for thought that openness to learning from multiculturalism makes people progress, and openness to appreciating the changing sense of identities with micro-globalization improves the power of identity. Over time, millions of migrants from other continents have made Australia home, enhanced cultural diversity, and expanded modern opportunities, which all result in a unique Australian identity. Still, it is based on one's lived experience to define the unique identity.

Traveling to Uluru/Ayers Rock, the large sandstone formation in the center of Australia, was exhilarating for me to tell modernization in Australia. It was winter August in Australia, and the weather was moderately cool. My first impression of Uluru/Ayers Rock was nothing less than a barren desert landscape. It's said that humans settled in the area more than 10,000 years ago. In seeing the massive sandstone closely, Uluru is pre-modern despite me being modern. A small number of local Anangu, the traditional Aboriginal owners of Uluru-Kata Tjuta National Park, still live in scattered communities across this scared non-Western site. They traveled the land and created everything of today during the creation period – the mountains, the valleys, the rivers, and the streams, all plant and animal life. For Anangu, they believe they are the direct descendants of these ancestral beings.

Uluru is notable for its changing color at different times of the day and year when it glows red at dawn and sunset. Modernization over the years in Australia has made multiculturalism prosper and created substantial losses for the spiritual significance of Indigenous Australians. Every year modern tourism in Uluru/Ayers Rock attracts hundreds and thousands of visitors from all over the world. This provides the bedrock of modernization to Australia – economic benefits. I was on my way to Kata Tjuta National Park on a shuttle bus. The arid scenery was non-Western for someone who is from Chinese modernization – blue mallee, desert oak, mulga tree, desert poplar, dingo, kangaroo, and thorny devil. I was wondering: did Anangu yearn for economic benefits just as people in modern cities? Would Uluru/Ayers become like Sydney and Melbourne one day?

Walking along the downtown of each city in modern Australia, I was enmeshed in such baffling languages as Persian, Arabic, Japanese, Korean, French, or Indonesian; I observed the social movements of resistance identities and project identities; I meditated the hustle and bustle of history around me. As of this writing in October 2023, the Indigenous Voice Referendum braces for a Yes/No single question about whether to change the Constitution to recognize First Peoples of Australia by establishing a body called the Aboriginal and Torres Strait Islander Voice.[27] There were bitterness and history. Although the historic referendum was unsuccessful, there is now the capacity for negotiation, participation, and hope. In relation to the question raised by the economist Paul Collier – do both migrants and the Indigenous of host societies come to see each other as members of a common society? – perhaps it is a sense of belonging in an incommensurable difference between conceptions and experiences captured by Indigenous groups and migrant cohorts.[28]

Since foods convey the basic cravings of humankind insofar as foods can push a person to identify themselves. My appetite for foods evolves with the interdependent diverse globalization. As we saw the remarkable economic contribution of "modernization with Chinese characteristics" to Western modern development set off by the free flow of people in Chapter 1, people-to-people exchanges are at the heart beyond identities. On one occasion, I had lunch with a friend at a Thai restaurant in Gold Coast, a waitress asked if my friend and I came from mainland China and used Little Red Book app (Xiao Hongshu, China's answer to Instagram, a social media and e-commerce platform for users to share lifestyles, shopping experiences, and creative content). The Thai restaurant was hoping to attract more Chinese customers by offering a 10 percent discount for Chinese who have uploaded their experience at this Thai restaurant on Little Red Book app. The waitress told us that the Thai restaurant needed a boost from the Chinese audience for the COVID economic recovery, and we were Asians supporting each other.

It goes without saying that multiculturalism and migration flourish beyond identities although individuals' identifications differ from culture to culture plus lived experience. But we should also think through identity politics in multiculturalism and modernization, as mentioned in Chapter 1. One can be an identity or multiple identities, yet one may not be part of the people under identity politics. In Charles Taylor's *Multiculturalism: Examining the Politics of Recognition*, the issue of multiculturalism is unlikely to compromise one identity for another. Thus, the issue of recognition is that letting equal value of different cultures survive and acknowledging the worth.[29] My legitimizing identity of being Chinese in the context of globalization instills in me a mantra of openness to modernizing identities. On this, modernity cannot be divorced from being open to globalization.

Notes

1 Fukuyama, Francis. *Identity: Contemporary Identity Politics and the Struggle for Recognition*. Profile Books, 2018, p. 164.
2 "About Migration." *International Organization for Migration*, UN Migration IOM, www.iom.int/about-migration. What Is the Indigenous Voice to Parliament, How Would It Work, and What Happens Next
3 "China's Internal Migrants." *Council on Foreign Relationships*, 14 May 2009, www.cfr.org/backgrounder/chinas-internal-migrants. Accessed 16 Aug. 2023.
4 Chan, Kam Wing. "Internal Migration in China: Integrating Migration with Urbanization Policies and Hukou Reform." *KNOMAD—Policy Note*, vol. 16, 2021, pp. 1–2.
5 "Main Data of the Seventh National Population Census." *National Bureau of Statistics of China*, 11 May 2021, www.stats.gov.cn/english/PressRelease/202105/t20210510_1817185.html. Accessed 9 Jan. 2024.
6 "'Destined to Disappear': The Last Generation of China's 'Bang-Bang Army.'" *The New York Times*, 28 June 2016, cn.nytimes.com/culture/20160628/china-chongqing-bang-bang/dual/. Accessed 16 Aug. 2023.
7 "'Destined to Disappear': The Last Generation of China's 'Bang-Bang Army.'" *The New York Times*, 28 June 2016, cn.nytimes.com/culture/20160628/china-chongqing-bang-bang/dual/.
8 "Catchphrases Etched in History." *China's 30 Years of Reform*, China Daily, 18 Dec. 2008, www.chinadaily.com.cn/30years/2008-12/18/content_7316538.htm. Accessed 16 Aug. 2023.
9 Zhao, Liqiu et al. "New Trends in Internal Migration in China: Profiles of the New-Generation Migrants." *China & World Economy*, vol. 26, no. 1, 2018, pp. 18–41, doi:10.1111/cwe.12227.
10 IOM UN. "World Migration Report 2022." 2022. https://worldmigrationreport.iom.int/wmr-2022-interactive/. Accessed 16 Aug. 2023.
11 IOM UN. "World Migration Report 2022." 2022. https://worldmigrationreport.iom.int/wmr-2022-interactive/. Accessed 16 Aug. 2023.Also see Natarajan, Anusha, et al. "Key Facts about Recent Trends in Global Migration | Pew Research Center." *Pew Research Center*, https://www.facebook.com/pewresearch, 16 Dec. 2022, https://www.pewresearch.org/short-reads/2022/12/16/key-facts-about-recent-trends-in-global-migration/#:~:text=The%20number%20of%20international%20migrants,Organization%20for%20Migration%20(IOM). Accessed 16 Aug. 2023.
12 Castelli, Francesco. "Drivers of Migration: Why Do People Move?" *Journal of Travel Medicine*, vol. 25, no. 1, 2018, doi:10.1093/jtm/tay040.
13 Fukuyama, Francis. *Identity: Contemporary Identity Politics and the Struggle for Recognition*. Profile Books, 2018, p. 164.

14 "2022 Population Statement." *Australian Government Center for Population*, https://population.gov.au/publications/statements/2022-population-statement. Accessed 5 Sept. 2023.

15 "Germany's Population Has Not Grown in 2020 for the First Time since 2011." *Statistisches Bundesamt*, 21 June 2021, https://www.destatis.de/DE/Presse/Pressemitteilungen/2021/06/PD21_287_12411.html. Accessed 16 Aug. 2023.

16 Statistics Canada. "The COVID-19 Pandemic Disrupted the Economic Integration of Many Immigrants." *Statcan.Gc.Ca*, 5 Dec. 2022, https://www150.statcan.gc.ca/n1/daily-quotidien/221205/dq221205b-eng.htm. Accessed 16 Aug. 2023.

17 "A New Wave of Mass Migration Has Begun." *The Economist*, 28 May 2023, https://www.economist.com/finance-and-economics/2023/05/28/a-new-wave-of-mass-migration-has-begun. Also see Australia's permanent migration planning program in 2023–2024 at "Migration Program Planning Levels." *Immigration and Citizenship Website*, https://immi.homeaffairs.gov.au/what-we-do/migration-program-planning-levels. Accessed 7 Sept. 2023.

18 Collier, Paul. *Exodus: Immigration and Multiculturalism in the 21st Century*. Penguin UK, 2013.

19 Collier, Paul. *Exodus: Immigration and Multiculturalism in the 21st Century*. Penguin UK, 2013, pp. 86–7, 107.

20 Collier, Paul. *Exodus: Immigration and Multiculturalism in the 21st Century*. Penguin UK, 2013, pp. 111–34. Also see Dumont, Jean-Christophe and Thomas Liebig. "Is Migration Good for the Economy." *Migration Policy Debates*. OECD Publishing, 2014.

21 Collier, Paul. *Exodus: Immigration and Multiculturalism in the 21st Century*. Penguin UK, 2013, p. 180.

22 World Bank Group. "Remittances Grow 5% in 2022, despite Global Headwinds." *World Bank Group*, 30 Nov. 2022, https://www.worldbank.org/en/news/press-release/2022/11/30/remittances-grow-5-percent-2022. Accessed 16 Aug. 2023.

23 OECD. *The Development Impact of Migration in Origin Countries*. 2016.

24 "Australian History." *Australianexplorer.com*, https://www.australianexplorer.com/australian_history.htm. Accessed 12 Sept. 2023.

25 Australian Bureau of Statistics. "Population: Census." *ABS*, 2021, https://www.abs.gov.au/statistics/people/population/population-census/latest-release. Also see "Multicultural Framework Review." *Department of Home Affairs*, 14 Oct. 2023, www.homeaffairs.gov.au/about-us/our-portfolios/multicultural-framework-review/about-the-multicultural-framework-review. Accessed 10 Jan. 2024.

26 Grant, Stan. "Stan Grant - Australia Is a Country Best Seen from Above." *British Council*, https://www.britishcouncil.org.au/crossing-points/stan-grant-australia-country-best-seen-above. Accessed 12 Sept. 2023.

27 Allam, Lorena. "What Is the Indigenous Voice to Parliament, How Would It Work, and What Happens Next?" *The Guardian*, 4 Sept. 2023, https://www.theguardian.com/australia-news/2023/sep/04/what-is-the-indigenous-voice-to-parliament-australia-what-does-it-mean-explained-referendum-campaign. Accessed 16 Aug. 2023.

28 In terms of Paul Collier's question, there has been scant research on Indigenous Australians' attitudes toward it, given the complexity of Indigenous issues in Australia. But I used this angle for the answer based on this ABC's article by Moreton-Robinson, Aileen. "'Our Story Is in the Land': Why the Indigenous Sense of Belonging Unsettles White Australia." *ABC Religion & Ethics*, 9 Nov. 2020, https://www.abc.net.au/religion/our-story-is-in-the-land-indigenous-sense-of-belonging/11159992. I think there is a need to conduct relevant annual research about Paul Collier's question: do both migrants and the Indigenous come to see each other as members of a common society?

29 Taylor, Charles. *Multiculturalism: Examining the Politics of Recognition*. ERIC, 1994.

4 Being Modern Dignity and Safety

The history of modernity is a history of Western progress. Modernity historically unfolds in Renaissance and Enlightenment, revolting against the stages between tradition and being modern. As the German philosopher Jürgen Habermas would say, modernity is an "unfinished project."[1] In dictionary, the word "modernity" refers to the quality or state of being modern that is different to all past forms of human experience. Hence, modernity is a social existence of humans that is significantly different from the past.[2]

All over the world, modernization is not less than one model. Modernization paradigm, however, is like a beacon for me to read micro realities, coming to understand economies, people, cultures, and identities in such a way that we live beyond identities in modernity. This is about being modern dignity and safety. To attend to human dignity is closely linked to the idea of human worth. More often than not, philosophy has extensively shed light on a bounty of conceptions of human dignity. The English philosopher Thomas Hobbes proposed "the public worth of a man, which is the value set on him by the commonwealth."[3] The Geneva-born philosopher Jean-Jacques Rousseau famously contended that "man is born free; yet everywhere we find him in chains."[4] The German Philosopher Immanuel Kant argued that persons were above all price, the virtue of an inner worth of a dignity admitted of no equivalent to human needs of a fancy price.[5] In defense of the narrative on identity of dignity, Francis Fukuyama holds that the inner self is embodied in thymos by using Hegel's philosophy that human history is a struggle for recognition.[6]

At all times dignity is uttered with safety in our modern public discourse. It is in dignity and safety that someone strives for basic survival needs and resources. It is in dignity and safety that migrants should be treated with respect and without exclusion. It is in dignity and safety that various social movements hope to realize demands. It is in dignity and safety that vulnerable groups need more protection. It is in dignity and safety that workers urge fair pay and a healthy work environment. It is in dignity and safety that humankind wishes to have a roof over one's head. These social actors may live with mixed identities around the world, and their motivations of demands are organically in dignity and safety.

DOI: 10.4324/9781003528180-5

In one sense, dignity and safety come to us through the articulation of life in connection with self, others, and the external world. In the work of the American philosopher Donald Davison, the three varieties of knowledge are empirically coordinate: knowledge of our own minds, knowledge of other minds, and knowledge of external realities.[7] This relational dimension then informs us that one's dignity and safety cannot be lost belonging to one's autonomous self, others' thoughts, and the wider world in us.

Likewise, the Brazilian educator Paulo Freire puts something to the effect that every human being is capable of educating each other in a dialogical encounter to name the world provided with proper tools, "he or she comes to a new awareness of self, has a new sense of dignity, and is stirred by a new hope."[8] With respect to micro realities, facts, and research, this chapter maintains to look beyond identities in terms of being modern dignity and safety in three sections: Identity Economics Influence, Daily Dignity and Safety, and Our Dreams.

Identity Economics Influence

The economist Keyu Jin highlights that the power of economic prosperity lies in its ability to change people's lives.[9] This is the bedrock of modernization in many parts of the world. For me as a new generation of Chinese, the extraordinary metamorphosis of economic miracle within China has changed the three varieties of knowledge that modernize identities and the changing sense of identities with micro-globalization for the new generation of Chinese; otherwise, I am not able to write this book without the three varieties of knowledge.

For a long time, people have sought to live comfortably in dignity and safety across the globe. And economics emphasizes the utility function when people make optimal decisions on how to spend money. Yet, not every individual is the same as everyone else. In their collaborative book *Identity Economics*, the American economists Rachel Kranton and George Akerlof discuss how our conception of who we are and who we choose to be may influence how hard we work as well as how we study, spend, and save.[10]

Body art is popular in the modern world, including tattoos, body piercing of ears, nose, navel, body painting, and dieting. We consider identity to change bodies and become an ideal. Cosmetic surgery is an answer to a modern pleasing ideal. Dubbed the world's plastic surgery capital, the South Korean cosmetic surgery industry accumulated a value of about 1.95 billion US dollars during 2018–2022.[11] To a degree, human beings are particular about identity choices, each of which is in a reciprocal relationship to economic satisfaction.

In the robust modern context of digital economy, hyper-connectivity establishes a suite of digital identities tucked behind in-person communication. Digital identity can be fake or real, but it is a fabric of being essentially human. The digital representation of ourselves allows us to adopt identity economics in the use of identity so that digital identity becomes profitable to secure online businesses. In the case of ID verification, a Mastercard identity in digital economy evaluates our real-time consumption and saving intentions, and you can track your identity economics as soon as possible to be modern dignity and safety.

More or less identity-related utility function is consciously bound to social settings, and the choices imply trade-offs and pay-offs. Occupations and gender reflect one of the social patterns of such identity economics with man and woman.[12] Women are viewed biologically less suitable for jobs in science and engineering that are tagged for men. In the social context of identity economics, workers have a sense of who they are in society and how they should behave. Labor demand yields labor supply for women and men. In this way, firms usually hire men for men's roles and women for women's roles. And employers maximize profits to pay wages and segregate gender.[13] In the situation of recruitment eligibility, professions occasionally require specific education levels and certification. Women are assumed in occupations with less human capital investment. By contrast, male professions are matched with more human capital investment.[14] With the way of modern thinking, this somewhat stimulates the commitment to Diversity, Equity, and Inclusion (DE&I) that more and more companies tend to adopt for business, bringing employees from different backgrounds together in a comfortable space with their identities.

If that being the case, identity is a limited choice for the self's dignity and safety vis-à-vis the social difference of identity economics in the modern world. Parents usually choose the best school to influence a child's future identification with others. Women are torn between an option to be a housewife or a career woman. The choice of where to buy a property can affect how people think of themselves. The decision is full of ambivalence and anxiety when immigrants choose to give up their original legal status and change other citizenships.

All too often, consumer behaviors are driven by cultural, social, personal, and psychological features to define a market. With identity economics, identity vis-à-vis marketing segmentation can be a deeper explanation of identity utility. Whichever group a person identifies with, the buying identity divides people into this or that group, driving people to make decisions that realize utility maximation. An interesting case is ticket fares in air travel. Targeting consumers who are looking for the cheapest way to travel, low-cost airlines usually provide affordable tickets to budget-conscious travelers. The pricing strategy does not include checked-in baggage, and people need to pay a little extra money for a full catering service experience. One's identity is the boarding ticket, so low-cost airlines charge excess baggage that costs almost the same price as a flight ticket. In this way, baggage is endowed with an identity. On account of identity economics influence, being a human is making identity trade-offs over identities in dignity and safety. At this moment, we are going to look at daily dignity and safety.

Daily Dignity and Safety

Dignity and safety for me means that under no harmful circumstances, hard work pays off in any modern society, and this faith is viable no matter how divergent identities inherently exist between you and me. And behaviors must abide by the rules of legitimizing identities. The knowledge of the self, of others' thoughts, of the wider world, shall be interdependent with one another within modernization paradigm. As a human desires more, so do dignity and safety multiply.

Dignity is not a modern word. Early Confucianism connected dignity to benevolence indicating care for people and desire the well-being of others to develop the worth of moral potential which is named acquired dignity. It also includes the idea of universal dignity that every human being is born with moral potential and thereby owns human dignity.[15] Beyond identities, the concept of dignity resonates with Western thought from ancient Greece attributable to Stoicism as "virtue" to the most famous modern philosophy in Immanuel Kant's *Groundwork for the Metaphysics of Morals during Enlightenment* in the eighteenth century – "Whatever has a price can be replaced by something else as its equivalent; on the other hand, whatever is above all price, and therefore admits of no equivalent has a *Würde* (Würde translated as dignity)."[16]As such, dignity is priceless in the course of history.

Safety has been emphasized with the evolution of modernization dating back to the First Industrial Revolution with the invention of technologies from the mid-eighteenth century. Arising out of technology advancement, the safety movement has come into being since the early 1900s in America when industrial accidents were commonplace.[17] The focus on safety rings true in all contexts of modernization to ensure technology is safe to create social change for dignified human lives.

Thus, dignity and safety are put together through the articulation of life in connection with self, others, and the external world. This time please immerse yourself in daily dignity and safety on the ground and associate them with yours as being modern dignity and safety.

International airports bear all the hallmarks of a little bit dignity and safety that identities come and go. It is my favorite place in each city to see through the small acts of dignity and safety when humans move around. International airports are the closest windows to globalization where the flows of goods and people magically pass through. Taking red-eye flights is literally an ordeal notwithstanding a full night's sleep. In order to minimize jet lag and squeeze in time for sightseeing, I book red-eye tickets for trips occasionally on purpose. Sometimes, I am lucky to stumble upon the beautiful glow of sunrise and sunset over the sky; sometimes, I am thrilled to browse the duty-free shops selling chic garments; sometimes, I am empathetic toward the ships passing in the night that make a decent living and guarantee human safety in the roles of taxi drivers, ground staff, and cabin crew. These early morning and late night scenes at international airports affirm how genuine down-to-earth humankind diligently earns dignity and safety, running on fumes to arrive at destinations. Although taxi fares are slightly expensive at night rates, the mutual knowledge between drivers and passengers is a testament to a sense of common purpose that we all want to safely get to our places and lead a dignified life for families.

Holding a handrail on the metro in the morning peak hour around the world, each compartment is packed out. The people are called passengers, but they have their own identities to clock in and clock out. Passengers are drowsy and bored. The identities they are working at are ones that bind them to dignity and safety for a life. Every one of us makes up our societies between West and East. Whether politicians or civilians, celebrities or common people, scientists or students, millionaires or homeless, city dwellers or villagers, white-collar or blue-collar workers, we are just striving for personal dignity and safety in different life cycles within modernization paradigm.

Securing daily dignity and safety involves quality education and health. The 2023 UNESCO data shows that over 240 million children and youth between the ages 6 and 18 worldwide still cannot access quality education enrolled in pre-primary, primary, secondary, or higher levels of education.[18] Sustainable Development Goal 4 insofar as aims to "Ensure inclusive and equitable quality education and promote lifelong learning opportunities for all."[19]

Every summer, more firefighters are on the frontlines of deadly wildfires all over the world. At the peak of the 2019–2020 Queensland bushfire season in Australia, firefighters battled more than 90 bushfires at once.[20] When I lived in UniLodge's student apartment, smoke detectors were occasionally triggered. The fire alarms reported the fire brigade in 10 minutes even at 1 a.m. By the time the Aussie firefighters arrived, they swiftly put on equipment and broke into doors to extinguish smoke, they knocked on every room to evacuate people beyond nationalities, and they made sure everyone was safe and sound. Firefighting is a dangerous role which fights for the dignity of fire crews themselves and the safety of people in fire. The calamity of fire teaches a lesson that human life's dignity is so precious over identity to ensure the safety of others.

Invisible in the eyes of leaders and citizens across the globe, sanitation workers perform pits maintenance, rubbish collecting, and fecal sludge transportation at the cost of safety, health as well as living conditions. This low-profile public service by sanitation workers safeguards others' health and safety at public toilets and garbage drop-off sites. Comparably, construction workers deliver safe housing for the public to shelter, and they speak up to improve decent working conditions through strikes. Underpinned by such daily dignity and safety, the agenda of Sustainable Development Goal 8 calls for "Promote sustained, inclusive and sustainable economic growth, full and productive employment and decent work for all."[21]

Resistance identities can be in conflict with legitimizing identities, morality, tradition, as well as modernization. The Indigenous movement, anti-globalization movement, Me Too movement, and many other movements of resistance identities oppose certain aspects of modern values. This is to be modern dignity and safety, come whatever may. On the one hand, biotechnology reverses the natural way of giving birth for human beings in terms of morality. On the other hand, biotechnology achieves lucrative businesses and improves human health in terms of dignity and safety.

As someone born and raised in Sichuan Province Southwest China, I have been an insider watching the daily dignity and safety on the abundant land shrouded in white mist. Fluent in the local Sichuan dialect enables me to communicate well with the way of Sichuan Chinese behaviors. In reflecting on daily dignity and safety in Sichuan Province Southwest China, I have been impressed with the street vendors living below the middle income by international standards who work around the clock and endeavor to earn decent wages to survive and thrive. These street vendors have no clue as to identity politics for dignity and safety, but they go the extra mile to do identity economics for a better life than "traditional" in Chinese modernization. The industrious resilience within the Chinese spirit is an invaluable pride in conjunction with my modern liberal thinking to cherish.

In the preceding chapter, what we have seen a flock of bang-bang porters to Chongqing is a search of humankind yearning for dignity and safety through hard work galvanized by identity economics influence. Every sweat bang-bang porters bear on the shoulders with a load of goods represents that persons shall be respectable price over fancy price. As modernization goes on, bang-bang porters and migrant workers assimilate China's booming food delivery industry. By 2021, food deliverymen in China numbered over 6 million. The average commission per order deserves as little as 0.68 cents.[22] Modern deliverymen are seen rushing on electric scooters with helmets, and the GPS-enabled food delivery app is everything to them. Many of them work more than 10 hours a day to just earn around 1000 US dollars per month.

My firsthand engagement with immigrants to Australia is all about the desires for human value and safe shelter in dignity and safety, of those who come from China, India, Japan, Greece, Vietnam, South Korea, and so on. Even the UAE, one of the world's top five richest countries with the greatest share of the international migrant population, is a sharp reminder of a scene where the super-rich come to stay in the luxury hotels and the super-poor come to work in them. A morning stroll at 6 o'clock in Dubai is a reflection of migrant construction workers who slave away at dignity and safety to be part of this hyper-modern wealth-divided society.

Being modern dignity and safety cannot get away from inclusive mental health achievement in that choices in a modern liberal society will also leave people unhappy and disconnected from their fellow human beings.[23] More than 70 percent of the world's population do not have access to mental health treatment care that they need.[24] This dignity and safety in mental health signals that solutions are supposed to break the barriers of self-stigma, low confidence, low self-esteem, and social isolation.[25] Dignity, safety, and mental health must go hand-in-hand for people worldwide without fear and inhibition in modernity.

Of course, as people become better off, their priority to meet basic needs gives way to longings for work-life balance and a wide range of high-quality lifestyles.[26] This is none other than the new generation of Chinese equipped with modern communication technologies and global consciousness that a proliferation of cravings for dignity and safety of employment, gender equity, international education, self-expression, and green consumption within modernization paradigm coupled with identity economics influence.

At the point of this writing, the third decade of the twenty-first century looks eerily unstable around the world. People are laboring under the burden of high inflation on everyday items from the United Kingdom to Argentina and Turkey to Australia as we are recovering from the coronavirus pandemic. Zeroing in on the realistic daily life, humans feel the pinch so that they choose to skip meals to save bills in exchange for a bit dignity and safety.[27] Wars can interrupt global supply chains, destroy infrastructures, and brutally displace people, but wars can refresh modernization stages and enhance technological advancement at the sacrifice of humanity. The ongoing wars in the twenty-first century may emotionally make sense of identity. Yet, the everyday demands for dignity and safety of decent wages and survival rise above a wealth of identities as humankind. Furthermore, we are moving to our dreams.

Our Dreams

The sun rises and sets day after day on Earth, and we are living on the same planet. Even mountains and seas cannot distance people with shared aspirations. The novel *Adventures of Huckleberry Finn* by the American author Mark Twain narrates a world in which Huck Finn lives and a world in which Huck Finn attempts to land, down the Mississippi River with a runaway slave Jim in search of their dreams against the American Dream while they reconcile identities over morality.

Over the course of modernization, the American Dream has been enthralling in the role of the Statue of Liberty which signifies hope and better opportunities for legitimizing American identity's prosperity and success by way of hard work, determination, and initiative. The American Dream incorporates both the macro vision for modern America writ large and individual components such as home ownership, freedom, ideal jobs, and being healthy. To other societies, the Australian Dream is a pragmatic belief that home ownership can bring about a better life and is a manifestation of success and security. The Chinese Dream is a changing discourse that embodies a collective consciousness of the legitimizing Chinese identity in addition to technological innovation and economic progress, and that is all along modernizing identities.

At any rate, identity economics influence has empirically echoed the public discourse of these Dreams that identity trade-offs affect how hard we work, how we study, spend, and save.

Our dreams converge probably there are opposing modernization models that cultivate identities in the company of globalization. Buying a property takes ages for a human to save up enough for a deposit. A property marks a space in which a person needs to find belonging in modernity, and this identity has been recognized as the quintessence of being a full human being. Evolving with opposite Westernization, more than 90 percent of households own a property in China, and over 20 percent of Chinese households own multiple properties.[28] A decent home for all remains a shared reality in Australia, America, the United Kingdom, and Europe. Homeownership rates of around 65 percent on average have coincided with cost-of-living crisis in the United Kingdom, Australia, America, and France at this time of writing in 2023 and 2024, which is a fading dream to ordinary people, particularly to Generation Z.[29] An Aussie friend told me that the crazily high housing price was rather intimidating for many ordinary people residing in Westernization to buy a place. With years of hard work in business, he was blessed to independently afford a house in an affluent suburb, and on a global scale, there were quite a few people fighting a homeownership mission for life in different societies within modernization paradigm.

In my talk with people about "what is your dream," the answers vary from person to person. The aspirations are equally to be better than "traditional." Some want to get rich and become an engineer, a professor, a manager, or a boss, and so on. Others pursue family, friendship, health, happiness, or reputation. The dreams are irrelevant to the modernization theory. Yet, the dreams motivate us to be modern dignity and safety.

As we saw earlier about the beginning of the safety movement, safety develops with modernization. Modern humans may have to accommodate identities in pursuit of dreams, and the identity by birth will be lost. This betokens a human history shaped by dignity and safety. In line with Confucianism and Western philosophy, Francis Fukuyama is right that there is a genetic endowment in every member of human species that allows one to become a whole human being, which distinguishes a human in essence from other creatures. The source of human dignity is founded on human genetics.[30] A dog has no concept of dignity, or his identity is named by a human with dignity. A safe and dignified life of a dog calls forth the highest good in man within modernization paradigm.

Financial security is considered a sign of confidence to accomplish survival expenses, traveling, as well as better education. The new generation of Chinese loves to spend and engage in dignified, safe, and cozy life values that align more closely with the young people in other countries. Their dreams are socially conscious and tangible concerning diversity, integrity, and environment for good.[31] The post-1990s generation including me grew up in more comfortable conditions and a more liberal global environment. The identities move with a high tide of migration, digital economy, as well as social movements of project identities. The dreams of the young are to choose identities; this is nothing but for a better tomorrow.

Modernization is accelerated by exponential technological change. Moore's Law by the co-founder of Intel, Gordon E. Moore, describes that the number of transistors on integrated circuits doubles roughly every two years and the price stays almost the same.[32] This anticipation has held true across the production of tech industry for more than half a century now. Thanks to this exponential push in microchips, smaller, cheaper, smarter, and more efficient robots, phones, watches, computers, as well as software come along and unleash our dreams. It is exciting to keep an eagle eye on the state-of-the-art technological products in the lead-up to the annual official release date of brands like Apple, Huawei, and Samsung. Every year on the opening sale day of Apple's new series, large crowds of people line up for hours outside the flagship stores throughout the world to get the latest devices. My generation is nothing short of jumping on the bandwagon for this dream. This seemingly produces a novel human Moore's Law: faster, newer, and smaller.

Deepened by modern communication technology and social media, modern identity terms metamorphose with waking minds and lived experience. This is why public relations are so important and widely practiced to ensure mutually beneficial relations building between organizations and individuals. Our identities entrenched in the power of identity just rapidly diffuse across groups through planned and deliberate identity dreams.

"What is your dream" is a simple question, yet it requires contemplation. The waking minds are not the wisdom of the sleeping minds. Dreaming during sleep aids us in conveying feelings and thoughts we cannot put into spoken language. Dreaming during sleep gives us a wonderland to exercise creative imaginations. Right now we are waking up to the insane reality that the only wish of children and adults in the war zones is to live. To be, or not to be, that is not the point. At every dream, your choice is about being true to who you are and who you will be.

Notes

1 Trainor, Brian. "The Origin and End of Modernity." *Journal of Applied Philosophy*, vol. 15, no. 2, 1998, pp. 133–144. Also see Habermas, Jürgen, and Seyla Ben-Habib.
2 Shilliam, Robbie. "Modernity and Modernization." *Oxford Research Encyclopedia of International Studies*, 2010, p. 1.
3 See Leviathan, Chapter X: Of Power, Worth, Dignity, Honour and Worthiness.
4 Rousseau, Jean-Jacques. *The Social Contract*. Penguin Books, 2004..
5 Debes, Remy. "A History of Human Dignity." Forum for Philosophy, 5 Feb. 2018, https://blogs.lse.ac.uk/theforum/a-history-of-human-dignity/. Accessed 8 Oct. 2023.
6 See Fukuyama, Francis. *Identity: Contemporary Identity Politics and the Struggle for Recognition*. Profile Books, 2018.
7 Davidson, Donald. "Three Varieties of Knowledge." *Royal Institute of Philosophy Supplements*, vol. 30, 1991, pp. 153–66, doi:10.1017/S1358246100007748.

8 Freire, Paulo et al. *Pedagogy of the Oppressed.* 50th anniversary edition ed., Bloomsbury Academic, 2018.
9 Jin, Keyu. *The New China Playbook: Beyond Socialism and Capitalism.* Swift Press, 2023, p. 23.
10 Akerlof, George A. and Rachel E. Kranton. *Identity Economics How Our Identities Shape Our Work, Wages, and Well-Being.* Course Book ed., Princeton University Press, 2010.
11 Akerlof, George A. and Rachel E. Kranton. *Identity Economics How Our Identities Shape Our Work, Wages, and Well-Being.* Course Book ed., Princeton University Press, 2010. Akerlof and Rachel's book touched upon the consideration of cosmetic surgery to change identity and become an ideal. I researched the data in South Korea. "South Korea Plastic Surgery Market Report and Forecast 2023–2028." *South Korea Plastic Surgery Market Size, Share, Analysis 2023–2028*, www.expertmarketresearch.com/reports/south-korea-plastic-surgery-market. Accessed 24 Sept. 2023.
12 Akerlof, George A. and Rachel E. Kranton. "Economics and Identity." *The Quarterly Journal of Economics*, vol. 115, no. 3, 2000, pp. 715–53, doi:10.1162/003355300554881.
13 Akerlof, George A. and Rachel E. Kranton. *Identity Economics How Our Identities Shape Our Work, Wages, and Well-Being.* Course Book ed., Princeton University Press, 2010, pp. 86–87.
14 Akerlof, George A. and Rachel E. Kranton. *Identity Economics How Our Identities Shape Our Work, Wages, and Well-Being.* Course Book ed., Princeton University Press, 2010, pp. 86–87.
15 Li, Yaming. "The Confucian Concept of Human Dignity and Its Implications for Bioethics." *Developing World Bioethics*, vol. 22, no. 1, 2022, pp. 23–33, doi:10.1111/dewb.12312.
16 Kant, Immanuel, and Jerome B. Schneewind. *Groundwork for the Metaphysics of Morals.* Yale University Press, 2002.
17 Palmer, Lew R. "History of the Safety Movement." *The Annals of the American Academy of Political and Social Science*, vol. 123, no. 1, 1926, 9–19.
18 "244m Children Won't Start the New School Year (UNESCO)." *UNESCO.Org*, 20 Apr. 2023, www.unesco.org/en/articles/244m-children-wont-start-new-school-year-unesco. Accessed 07 Oct. 2023.
19 "Goal 4: Quality Education." *The Global Goals*, 17 Sept. 2021, https://www.globalgoals.org/goals/4-quality-education/. Accessed 12 Nov. 2023.
20 Sheehan, Amy, et al. "420 Bushfires in Days Exhaust Firefighters and 'worst Fire Season in 70 Years' Is Just Beginning." *ABC News*, 27 Oct. 2023, www.abc.net.au/news/2023-10-28/qld-bushfire-season-worst-in-70-years/103032562. Accessed 12 Nov. 2023.
21 "Goal 8: Decent Work and Economic Growth." *The Global Goals*, 17 Sept. 2021, https://www.globalgoals.org/goals/8-decent-work-and-economic-growth/. Accessed 12 Nov. 2023.
22 "How China's Delivery Drivers Quietly Fight to Improve Their Lot." *The Economist*, The Economist Newspaper, 2 Nov. 2023, www.economist.com/china/2023/11/02/how-chinas-delivery-drivers-quietly-fight-to-improve-their-lot. Accessed 12 Jan. 2024.
23 See Fukuyama, Francis. *Identity: Contemporary Identity Politics and the Struggle for Recognition.* Profile Books, 2018, p. 165. Fukuyama indicates people can feel unhappy and disconnected in modernity, and I relate it to mental health that all societies are facing.
24 Wainberg, Milton L. et al. "Challenges and Opportunities in Global Mental Health: A Research-to-Practice Perspective." *Current Psychiatry Reports*, vol. 19, no. 5, 2017, pp. 28–28, doi:10.1007/s11920-017-0780-z.

25 "Dignity in Mental Health." *WHO*, 8 Oct. 2015, https://www.who.int/southeastasia/news/detail/08-10-2015-dignity-in-mental-health. Accessed 12 Nov. 2023.

26 Jin, Keyu. *The New China Playbook: Beyond Socialism and Capitalism.* Swift Press, 2023, p. 299.

27 Inflation remains high from northern hemisphere to southern hemisphere, and humans choose to skip meals in these nations. I select this article as a guide to observe micro realities. "New Study Reveals an Alarming Amount of Aussies Are Skipping Meals to Make Ends Meet." *News.com.au*, 24 Sept. 2023, https://www.news.com.au/finance/money/costs/new-study-reveals-an-alarming-amount-of-aussies-are-skipping-meals-to-make-ends-meet/news-story/4debf1722c791ae7695ef7800d287dfd. Accessed 12 Nov. 2023.

28 Huang, Y. et al. "Introduction to Si: Homeownership and Housing Divide in China." *Cities*, vol. 108, 2021, p. 102967, doi:10.1016/j.cities.2020.102967.

29 The homeownership rate in Australia is 67%, America 65.9%, the UK 65%, and France below 70%.

Van Onselen, Leith. "Home Ownership Now a Pipe Dream for Ordinary Australians." *MacroBusiness*, 24 July 2023, https://www.macrobusiness.com.au/2023/07/home-ownership-now-a-pipe-dream-for-ordinary-australians/. Accessed 12 Nov. 2023. Taylor, Mia. "Homeowner Data and Statistics 2023." *Bankrate*, Bankrate.com, 24 July 2023, https://www.bankrate.com/homeownership/home-ownership-statistics/. Accessed 12 Nov. 2023. Hilber, Christian. "How Can We Make Homes More Affordable?" *British Politics and Policy at LSE*, 24 May 2023, https://blogs.lse.ac.uk/politicsandpolicy/how-can-we-make-homes-more-affordable/. Accessed 12 Nov. 2023. Chocron, Véronique. "Homeownership in France: A Fading Dream." *Le Monde*, Le Monde, 11 Sept. 2023, https://www.lemonde.fr/en/opinion/article/2023/09/11/homeownership-in-france-a-fading-dream_6132338_23.html. Accessed 12 Nov. 2023.

30 Fukuyama, Francis. *Our Posthuman Future: Consequences of the Biotechnology Revolution.* Profile Books, 2002, pp. 171–4.

31 Dr. Keyu Jin has made insightful comments on the new generation of Chinese. I link her perspective with my experiences as a new generation of Chinese. Jin, Keyu. "An Interview with Keyu Jin." *Project Syndicate*, 23 May 2023, https://www.project-syndicate.org/onpoint/an-interview-with-keyu-jin-new-china-playbook-chinese-tech-innovation-2023-05. Accessed 14 Nov. 2023.

32 Max Roser. et al. "What Is Moore's Law?" *Our World in Data*, 28 Mar. 2023, https://ourworldindata.org/moores-law. Accessed 14 Nov. 2023.

5 The Power of Being

In the modern era of diffusion, power is no longer an abstract concentration in conversation. Rather, power is circulated as wealth, information, images, resources, and identities in global networks. It never disappears. In the words of the Spanish sociologist Manuel Castells, "Power still rules society; it still shapes, and dominates us."[1] As we saw in Chapter 2, identities have the power to build interests and values around experiences and refuse to succeed in orthodox practices. Thus, where there is identity, there is power. Identities, in a way, anchor the power for being modern dignity and safety.

While Francis Fukuyama sticks to a process of *isothymia* over *megalothymia* for recognition-based identities in modernity, the desires to be superior and to be recognized as equally good as everyone in society are, in effect, a reality of the power of being. In other words, it is power relations that drive humankind to progress in dignity and safety instead of recognition per se. And Manuel Castells deals with social movements attributed to identity, but on a deeper observation, that is all about the power of being. Why? Because humans are naturally a blank sheet of paper, and our demands are empowered by seeking modern dignity and safety. Such empowerment is translated to power relations which are the DNA of modernization. As claimed by Manuel Castells, "whoever has power shapes the institutions that regulate society in terms of its interests and values."[2]

In *Collins Dictionary*, the definition of power is the capacity to influence, act, compete, control, and dominate within resources. It is an uncountable noun. As such, power is unlimited. A great deal of our material needs or profile status is a desire for power to do things and influence others. Those who admire the roles of political power, C-suites, senior managers, top elites, and show stars, are in fact a desire for power as leadership to dominate. To be recognized as equally good as everyone in any society is a desire for power to compete with others. Recognition is not the key to identity; what Indigenous people genuinely ask for is the power to control sovereignty and domination in dignity and safety. A desire for power sharing to a degree empowers identity-featured social movements like feminism and Net Zero. In a sense, the power of being is borderless beyond identities. We all crave power. Right?

DOI: 10.4324/9781003528180-6

However, it hinges upon what kind of power and how powerful one chooses to be. The connection between recognition and economic power was well responded by Adam Smith in his *The Theory of Moral Sentiments*:

> Vanity is always founded upon the belief of our being the object of attention and approbation.
>
> The rich man glories in his riches, because he feels that they naturally draw upon him the attention of the world, and that mankind are disposed to go along with him in all the agreeable emotions with which the advantages of his situation so readily inspire him... The poor man, on the contrary, is ashamed of his poverty. He feels that it either places him out of sight of mankind, or, that if they take any notice of him, they have, however, scarce any fellow-feeling with the misery and distress which he suffers.[3]

This early modern insight contingently reveals that recognition is relative to the demand for economic power, and the identity of being rich, or poor, could motivate a person to seek a level of power, which is not some absolute level of wealth. For instance, if someone would like to be admitted to a top elite university, one must prove extraordinary power of eligibility. Considering the identity of being rich, or poor, the rich man is more likely to accept the offer than the poor man to go for the power of knowledge. More identities, more power. Identities, in a way, anchor the power for being modern dignity and safety.

Putting aside identities, the power of being is run after by each individual far and wide in every disparate modernity. Power relations are not largely constructed in the human mind, but they are empirically the talk "to be better." For the time being, communication networks implement globalization via human messages. Communication for Social Change/Development is to structure power changes. The power of being resides in power relations in all domains of our everyday realities. Without further ado, this chapter delves into the power of being – Power is Everywhere, Knowledge is Power, and the Lens of the "Power Cube."

Power Is Everywhere

What is your first automatic impression of the picture in Figure 5.1? The perception would be fixed on malnutrition in the Global South judging from the boy and the fridge. This is off the point. Please look closely at the fridge. As we all know, a fridge is used to help food stay fresh longer in cold temperatures. But this fridge was of no use for residents in the Irula tribe of Southern India. The darkness did not prevail in the homes of Irula tribal communities until 2016 after the installation of streetlights, not to speak of connections to appliances. Obviously, a lack of electric power wasted this fridge. There ought to be power wiring up the fridge so that communication is made for social

Figure 5.1 Photograph by Associate Professor Pradip Ninan Thomas with personal permission. It was one of the slides in my Master study's lectures on New Theorizing in CSC. The picture was taken by Associate Professor Pradip Thomas at the University of Queensland when he was doing work on mobile phone/laptop access among "tribal" communities in Southern India.

change in people's lives. We seek basic expenses yet never think beyond the power of being, that is power. In the context of poor infrastructure access, people have to become inventive and innovative. In India, the Hindi word "jugaad" is used to describe such DIY inventiveness. Once power supply is in the hands of people, residents have scope to use appliances in their capacity and make most use of electronic devices (see Figure 5.2).

The accent on being modern dignity and safety is common to many parts of the world. And measures tied to universal education, the rule of law, the enjoyment of freedom, as well as social housing have resulted in a quality of life, the betterment of humans and society. There are certainly merits in identities that give you advantages over the merits of achievement-based individualism, such that modernization glosses over the ways in which power is exercised, overlooks the facilitation of identities in power relations as the DNA of modernization given that in all contexts around the world, our cultural and social capital play an instrumental role in our life chances. At the macro level, the power that movers and shakers exert is exceptionally attractive to inspire dreams everywhere. At the micro level, the power that an ordinary person aspires to acquire is underlying dignity and safety. In some parts of the world, the fruits of modernization are distributed through power sharing. In other parts, modernization persistently transforms tradition through the enduring asymmetries of power.

In the influential work *An Essay Concerning Human Understanding*, it was John Locke who put forward the idea that individuals were born empty

Figure 5.2 A laptop being charged directly from the main electricity box. Photograph by Associate Professor Pradip Ninan Thomas at UQ with personal permission.

of rules, but individuals populate their identities and knowledge only from later experiences.[4] For all that we live in West or East, the power of being attached to power relations around us is very different from what you and I desire. Because children innately had no clue about power relations, empiricism develops humankind's power relationships based on experience, and identities are nurtured at the same time – therefore, power relations are altered with experiences anchored by identities. In the corporate world, a dream job is regarded as a means to an end, and it could denote a greater value of a human with a higher salary and respectable praise. In this sense, recognition is a fraction of the power of being. The more senior roles you are in, the more power you will have in rubbing shoulders with your counterparts and people at higher levels. This corporate power of being correspondingly applies to any other context that you think of.

To justify my observation that power is everywhere in this section, I borrow from the French philosopher Michel Foucault's hugely thought-provoking concentration on micro-powers exercised at the level of daily life. For Foucault, power is what makes us what we are. In my words, that is the power of being. In opposition to the conventional wisdom that power generates domination, coercion, and suppression, Foucault tells us that power operates on our very bodies, producing desirable types of bodies, thereby subjugating ourselves. Let me put it understandably, being powerful is carried out in a body. On the one hand, a human body achieves an autonomous identity and caloric energy by creating desires, and it needs nutrition to grow the reality of skills, consciousness, and ideality. On the other hand, the body of a society constitutes a network of institutions, relations, hierarchy, and resources for the functioning of a state.

As of 2023, the world's population has surpassed 8 billion. We live longer and enjoy healthier lives than at any other point in human history. But power persists with diversified identities in communities and organizations, which manipulates bodies to mobilize the acquisition of power. Power relations are faced with complex identities when it comes to being modern dignity and safety. The reality is that people of different identities prize certain values over others, and their bodies regulate power for prosperity, stability, security, or freedom along with being modern dignity and safety. In writing this, I pick one Chinese household idiom that runs prominently through the power of being, it would be this: "Humankind struggles upwards, water flows downwards (人往高处走, 水往低处流 ren wang gao chu zou, shui wang di chu liu)." Modern humans always seek to fly high and make progress for a better life, so the power of being should serve as the power to honor one's body.

Pundits and social reality also give us a perspective that power can meet with resistance. Foucault was of the view that power continued and manifested itself in the new ways against resistance: "Power, after investing itself in the body, finds itself exposed to a counterattack in the same body…it can retreat here, re-organize its forces, invest itself elsewhere…and so the battle continues."[5] Fast forward to human activities around digital communication networks in the twenty-first century, Manuel Castells empirically observes that wherever is power there is resistance to power, and the exercise of power induces counterpower. As we've learned in Chapter 2, resistance identities are unsatisfied with orthodox or legitimizing identities. Between modern headlines and realities, resistance identities are negotiations of power to accommodate interests of people to demand pay rise, female empowerment, participation, peace, and social justice, so to speak.

Modernization teaches us that to be better is to eat well, sleep well, and live well. With a new way of understanding power, modernization can evaluate human body and the power of being that human body reacts to the interplay of identities and power. Modern hospitals come out to address contemporary physical health and mental health. Just take a closer look at a horde of people at modern hospitals, a growing number of modern humans feel under the weather for the reason that modern life is way too fast-paced, hyper-connected, and superbly convenient. By virtue of eyes glued on screens in these information-networked days, there is an increased risk of health disorders with symptoms like headache, insomnia, panic, and eye strain to such an extent that body and the power of being clash with each other to become our identities.

Generation Z worldwide typically bears the brunt of power to rule body in the hope of the human rights to choose the identities and the values they live by. Compounded by the mounting cost of living and an uncertain future, the omnipresent reluctance to give birth among the new generation across the globe pushes my generation to fight with a body around identities juggling the power of being. Here are a couple of the current global trends. Lately, a survey data of 2000 participants conducted by Cash Lady, a UK-based financial services company, has discovered that almost half of participants in the United Kingdom confess that they plan to take a pass on having children and prioritize their own power of being – happiness.[6] Also in China, an online survey of 20,000 participants in 2022 pointed out that two-thirds of Chinese Generation Z respondents would decide against having children.[7] The falling fertility rates in America is a new history. A Pew Research Center's poll in 2021 found that 44 percent of people younger than 50 said they were opting out not to foster future generations.[8] This is modernization happening between East and West.

It is literally free will to empower the power of being. Free will certainly reinforces individual creativity. Free will is not alone, it is workable with power, body, and varying external contexts. To select food is free will to eat, but there is no free lunch. The human body as an autonomous identity sends a signal to order food, which then directs one's economic power to empower consumption. Additionally, in today's many modern places, food orders can be completed only if power lights up kitchens, wires up to card payment machines, and connects to the Internet. Recent life in China is astonishingly powerful in everything that operates from QR codes with your body's control on a smartphone and face-scanning through your body. In the late 1970s, biopower was coined by Michel Foucault who brought up the conception that the power of technology would manage humans and allow for the control of entire populations, and the subjugation of bodies. Nonetheless, modernization is not unchanging, so much so that identities carry with power in dignity and safety. Having been modernized identities and globalized identities, the new generation everywhere is in a position to use technology invented by human body. Hence, "mutual biopower" is more suitable for the template of our everyday modern lives: power over body, and body over power. Eventually, body controls power which connects our identities, whereas power manages humans for the power of being.

Power in the twenty-first century is a marathon that innovation comes from. Electronic vehicles have been unveiled since the second decade of the twenty-first century. The power competition is not only for car manufacturers around the world especially in China and America but also for heads of state who maintain power and foster talents. If we turn back the clock to the beginning of the twenty-first century, vehicles were simply the result of the Second Industrial Revolution from the late nineteenth century to the early twentieth century. Power, in a way, makes a difference in human lives within modernization paradigm.

Not everyone is at the same modernization stage in all societies and under all circumstances. First, power relations are not equal as we will discuss the lens of the "power cube" later. Second, the diversity of identities proceeds to achieve power to survive and thrive based on lived experience. Identity co-exists with power, and power begets honor, respect, and praise. Be that as it may, there are wins and losses of power that individuals and communities grapple with the power of being. The popular Chinese proverb "No sooner has a person left than a cup of tea cools down (人走茶凉 ren zou cha liang)" metaphorically mirrors the theme on that. When a person loses power, he/she loses praise, respect, or flattering as well. Accordingly, the power of being is fragile.

Knowledge Is Power

Ever since a student goes to school from day one, parents and teachers often instruct a maxim that "knowledge is power." Believe it or not, knowledge is the stepping-stone filled with questions and answers to individual thoughts, scientific study, or practical skills through education and communication – deepening human capital to social capital. It not only guides fame, money, occupation, and identity per person but also builds demographic structure, economic growth, technological innovation, and professional employment in each modern society. In a word, power comes from knowledge. Colloquially, knowledge is translated from experiences.

Let us delve into the maxim. The notable quote "Knowledge is power" is attributed to the English philosopher Francis Bacon's *Meditationes Sacrae* ("ipsa scientia potestas est").[9] The words did not disclose how powerful knowledge is unless we put it into perspective. In Chapter 4, we have read through our dreams to be modern dignity and safety. If one's dream is to accommodate identities in being modern dignity and safety, the power of being results from the knowledge of the dream. Hence, the knowledge one commands must be related to the field in order that he/she can achieve the dream. Typically, educational modernization pumps theories into our brains to integrate knowledge into experiences under assignment and assessment. This is no mere certification. The result of knowledge through educational modernization can bring out the best of people. Top grades will prepare "winners" for continued high-profile attention from talent acquisition teams, and low grades will probably not be progressed further in a time of modern talent race. Knowledge thereby sits on top of a throne above power, which internalizes knowledge.

It is with knowledge that we conceive of power to facilitate positive social change, help people in need, and update modernization forward. No wonder contemporary educational institutions establish mottos pertinent to power/knowledge over their purposes. My alma mater the University of Queensland displays the motto "Scientia ac Labore" (by means of knowledge and hard work) so as to show excellence in education creating change. The most remarkable celebration of the University of Queensland (UQ) has been the incredible invention of the human papillomavirus (HPV) vaccine which saves millions of lives around the world from cervical cancer, with Australia on track to be the first country to eliminate cervical cancer by 2035.[10] UQ's Professor Ian Frazer and Dr. Jian Zhou had only dreamed of a result of ridding cervical cancer when they set out to learn about HPV. With knowledge and tireless hard work, it turned out that the vaccine (Gardasil 9) is extremely powerful to protect against 90 percent cervical cancers in women and most of genital cancers in men caused by HPV infection. Today, the administered HPV vaccine doses have exceeded 270 million globally, and the power/knowledge is fueling the next generation's "knowledge is power."[11] Dear readers, please relate "knowledge is power" to your alma mater.

To critically appreciate the wisdom of power/knowledge, Michel Foucault has served as an inspiration on this front. Foucault's power/knowledge legacy imbues us with a central theme in social sciences vis-à-vis power and knowledge within modernization paradigm. In *The History of Sexuality*, power is always a function of knowledge to utilize knowledge. And knowledge is always an exercise of power that recreates its own field of power through knowledge.[12] Simply speaking, our knowledge is piling up rather than petering out to acquire power and earn identities. A case in point is education level categories from primary to secondary, from vocational to tertiary, from undergraduate to postgraduate, and PhD, resulting in the award of an academic degree of Bachelor, Master, or Doctor. After earning an academic identity, modern people apply the power/knowledge to their fields and regain new power in the way of promotions, reputations, and professional awards through knowledge.

Power/knowledge rapidly develops information and networks in effect. The everyday explosive information exchanges via social media are noisy to manipulate people's behavioral change. In a certain sense, knowledge is a matter of possession, and power is a matter of retention. Manuel Castells has forcefully analyzed that power can be exercised through the processes of communication that are played out in the global network planet.

Let us be down-to-earth with the exploration of power/knowledge within modernization paradigm. Though we need an enabling macro environment of power to cultivate modernization discourse, the greatest minds that have made a difference to modernization are not at least political power. Admittedly, political power is a never-ending cause for people who cling to radical social change and fancy public attention between East and West. However, the better modern social changes are created by innovative minds who set their eyes on micro realistic scenarios. Steve Jobs said, "We started out to get a computer in the hands of everyday people, and we succeeded beyond our wildest dreams."[13] A lot of people in the world own an iPhone throughout the third decade of the twenty-first century, and the possession of electronics knowledge reproduces the knowledge of information. Further, the knowledge of information communicates power relationships in different network societies within modernization paradigm yet not all global because competition exists in "knowledge is power."

In the previous section, we were impressed by Hindi DIY innovativeness and inventiveness in which people catch up with power in the context of poor infrastructure access. So, we can say that everyday power and knowledge are inextricably intertwined with respect to being modern dignity and safety. Another side of micro power/knowledge scenario regarding project identities would flag a question – who is the most powerful entity in the world? As a group of communities are poised to either transform energy production or declare campaigns for zero emissions, Mother Nature is put into power/knowledge. Mother Nature can mercilessly kill off dreams – flood, bushfire, heatwave, or snowstorm. We employ human's possession of knowledge to tackle the power of Mother Nature confronted with climate change, loss of biodiversity, air pollution, rising sea level, dwindling natural beauties, and waste disposal.

In terms of power retention, it literally means the power to retain one's power in any condition. Still, the reality is fragmented into multi-layered forms of power that we will be coming to understand in the next part from the lens of the "power cube." Under the modern sky, the possession of knowledge works for the retention of power across the areas of political institutions, business organizations, educational groups, and daily consumption. All this is to say that power/knowledge is trickling down.

In these modern days, a host of people feel uncertain about "knowledge is power" when unemployment rate keeps rising here and there. In order to make it, the highly educated new generation of Chinese is restless for expected jobs that match their degrees, yet "knowledge is power" leaves behind Chinese economic modernization. In Australia, high interest rates and inflation only motivate people to do sidelines being modern dignity and safety. And student loans are not out of the woods in Europe and America in Western modernization to put on a par with "knowledge is power."

In the end, "knowledge is power" can be dangerous too. This depends on two factors to facilitate. The first is the morality of identities since each person is unique in being modern dignity and safety whereby expands the demands for the power of being. Therefore, there are those who are vying for dominance by spreading misinformation and disinformation, pitting one against the other in modernity. The second is the approach to power/knowledge for whom and for what. Given power is everywhere as outlined just now, it is controversial to appreciate nuclear power, drug trade, money laundering, and biotechnology with the wisdom of hindsight in an age of accelerating modernization.

All in all, "knowledge is power" is not a static maxim. It evolves with modernization and identity for whom and for what. But next in this respect, it is crucial that we visit the lens of the "power cube" to have a nuanced understanding of the power of being.

The Lens of the "Power Cube"

> If we do not know the forms of power in the network society, we cannot neutralize the unjust exercise of power. And if we do not know who exactly the power-holders are and where to find them, we cannot challenge their hidden, yet decisive domination.[14]
>
> *Manuel Castells, Communication Power, p. 431*

Questions of haves and have-nots, and of the connections between power and powerlessness have been ongoing discussions at political institutions, many of which catalyze ambitious people to get promoted and attain power. For all that power is studied scholarly in a growing body of literature on political science and social sciences, it is too theoretical and abstract to apply to micro realities. My view is that a nuanced understanding of the power of being will attend to power through the lens of the "power cube" beyond identities.

While the lens of the "power cube" approach seems to be more accessible to academics in jargon, readers can grasp points of the forms of power associated with their real lives. For this, I would share my takeaway from the political sociologist John Gaventa's work based on the lens of the "power cube" in combination with my observations from the micro realities. The use of "power cube" is relevant to a broad range of fields, including trade, health, housing, digital inclusion, environmental issues, social movements, and natural resources. Leaving political considerations aside, the lens of the "power cube" in this book explores the topics – economic empowerment, education, and communication – upon power relationships with relevance to modernization paradigm.

John Gaventa goes great lengths to analyze the participation of power and powerlessness which situated inequality to the concentration of economic wealth vis-à-vis political power in 1980 in the book *Power and Powerlessness: Quiescence & Rebellion in an Appalachian Valley.* The prevailing argument is that power is exercised both in the public sphere and through hidden means, which inhibits the participation of the powerless and causes an unequal status quo.[15] In a word, power relations are not equal. Decades on, Gaventa and Martorano revisit the links between inequality, power, and participation, using the lens of the "power cube" approach. Power inequality is influenced by invisible forms of power from local to global, shaping the rules of individuals' aspiration to participate.[16]

Similar patterns of inequality creep up in a range of issues of poverty and growth, education, and environment in a way that the Sustainable Development Goals (SDGs) 10 aims to reduce inequality within and among countries.[17] To our knowledge, reducing inequality is championed under the umbrella of inclusiveness by a slew of communities and individuals. However, the root of inequalities at local, national, and global level is deep in the configurations of power as where there is identity, there is power. Power relations are unequal. Thus, those changemakers who wish to reduce inequality and create positive social change should, in fact, change power relations with their existing power. Otherwise, the patterns of inequality are left for generation after generation. To this, we must understand the power of being through the lens of the "power cube." And the power of being is in this sense about participation.

From a Communication for Development/Social Change perspective, power is the nature of participation, including power over, power with, and power from within, which is the sheer talk about power. Drawing from the "power cube" (see Figure 5.3), power is the interactivity of the forms, levels, and spaces of power. And the three dimensions completely reconnect our perceptions of power to micro realities and the development of the power of being.

First and foremost, the forms of power are characterized as observable and unobservable. These three forms of power probably map inequality onto participation. Visible power is what can be seen in a more transparent process – everyone can see the dominant actors. Hidden power may exercise control through certain key actors to cover up issues in the public arena – they keep people from engaging. Invisible power affects people's psychological feelings of an issue for action in which one is not able to be aware of his/her rights and interests that are hidden due to dominating values and behaviors of the powerless themselves – people may take powerlessness for granted with false consciousness.[18]

Economic empowerment in the context between community and political institutions, for example, involves various stakeholders from macro to grassroots in a program. In the modern world, policymakers say what measures to be carried out in conjunction with fulfilling economic performance for the best interests of all. This is hidden power without the engagement of the financially disadvantaged and the program executives. The executives do have visible power to implement the program. But the financially disadvantaged groups may consider the economic inequality as a circumstance in which their power is the internalization of dominant actors and key actors in society – the

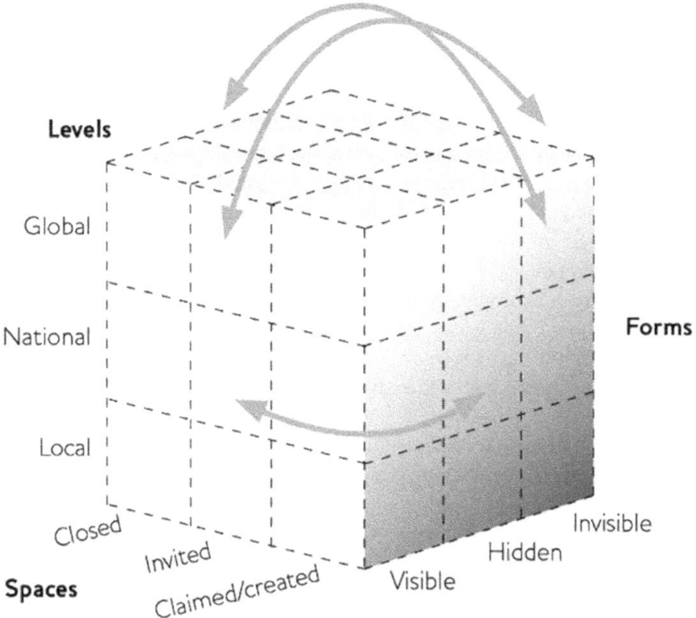

Figure 5.3 The power cube: the levels, spaces, and forms of power.

Source: Gaventa, John and Bruno Martorano. "Inequality, Power and Participation – Revisiting the Links." IDS bulletin (Brighton. 1984), vol. 47, no. 5, 2016, p. 15, doi:10.19088/1968-2016.164. Also see https://www.powercube.net/

disadvantaged with invisible power have to depend on visible power and hidden power to change the status quo. Or the less powerful people may be inclined to believe that being more powerful than the rich is unattainable to them, which curbs the aspirations of the powerless.

Beyond identities, almost 700 million people live in extreme poverty (with incomes less than 2.15 US dollars per day) throughout the world. According to the World Bank, global poverty reduction is off track at the mid-point of the SDGs and will be unlikely to meet the goal of ending extreme poverty by 2030 with an estimation of nearly 600 million people struggling in extreme poverty by then.[19] Seeing from the lens of the "power cube," if we do wholeheartedly change the power relations between the powerful rich and the powerless poor, that would fundamentally change economic empowerment from the beginning of participation, namely, what the powerless in poverty really want.

Of course, the forms of power can be found in all spaces of participation such as school classes, community meetings, social events, or public gatherings. It is important to link the forms of power to the levels and spaces of power as to how power is used, and who has power.[20] The levels of power range from micro household level to national and global levels. The outstanding features of globalization at scale and speed tend to escalate imbalanced power, giving rise to inequalities in economic and educational modernization. Power in a national space can mediate inequality in light of the pattern of modernization stage. Contrary to Westernization, power in the national space of "modernization with Chinese characteristics" has lifted 800 million Chinese people out of extreme poverty (people with incomes below 1.90 US dollar per day) over the past 40 years as highlighted by the World Bank and recognized by most counterparts in the West.[21] But power in local spaces amplifies inequality going forward – around 600 million Chinese have yet to join the monthly income above 300 US dollars in the 400 million middle-income group – well below the advanced-economy by the power of a global standard.[22]

Finally, the lens of the "power cube" suggests that the forms of power and levels of power cooperate with the spaces of power for participation. Closed spaces make decisions behind the closed doors of elites or people with relatively powerful capital. To protect tax peeks into transparent spaces that seek participation from all – such example we have seen with the penalties of tax evasion behaviors strengthened in each society's macro legal enforcement no matter who you are. The Panama Papers have revealed the extent to which the powerful rich and politicians around the world can exploit secretive wealth behind the scenes in which power and money are interconnected.[23] Other examples of closed spaces vis-à-vis power relations can also be reflected in the secrecy of community issues, referendum decisions, and social connections.

Against closed spaces, people are proactive to take action in their claimed/created spaces with a struggle of resistance identities, whether the acts be small-scale or large-scale social movements. Many of claimed/created spaces of power are connected to issues of inequality and empowerment.[24] In the power of being, the power of identity has a meaning in claimed/created spaces linked to power relations. As we are experiencing modernization in the twenty-first century, a surge of social movements engages in communication technologies to build visible power via user-generated content on online chat forums, petitions, or campaigns. *The World Social Science Report 2016: Challenging Inequalities: Pathways to a Just World* points out that inequalities should be tackled in terms of an interdisciplinary agenda that spans across economic, social, political, cultural, environmental, spatial, and knowledge dimensions. And the opening spaces of power for collective action by people are additional inclusive solutions to inequality.[25]

It is clear that communication is the project of modernization whose contested power relations seldom change. Internationally, Communication for Development is the transfer of aid in the orientation of modernization from developed countries to developing countries. With the combination of "knowledge is power," power in communication is both a resource and a strategy that are to project knowledge shaping, knowledge making, and behavioral changes.

Communication for Development is shaped by the power of national level that plays out alongside forms and spaces of power within modernization paradigm. In a world of Communication for Development/Social Change, no society is completely disconnected from the power of national level, the power of closed space, as well as the power of hidden form. Regardless of identities and media ownership form, Communication for Development/Social Change has to adapt to a dominant logic of national power. While China's framework for communications development is centrally controlled by the power of national level, the state, its economic decentralization at local levels consolidates the Chinese communications market and digital convergence that have made China establish the world's largest Internet market by 2014 to empower the local power of the Chinese people in their created spaces, albeit global digital communication disengagement.[26] The case in Indonesia reflects state's centralization connected with media conglomerates – Chairul Tanjung (CT Corp), Hary Tanoesoedibjo (Global Mediacom), Eddy Sariaatmadja (Emtek), Bakrie Group (Visi Media Asia), Surya Paloh (Media Group), and the Riady family (Berita Satu Media Holding), while also registering the power of global digital communication platforms. Conglomerates run the agendas of their political allies, and a couple of new platforms are backed by established media conglomerates as well.[27] Communication for Development in Mexico is greatly centralized and deeply marketized. Eighty percent of the power of radio stations' ownership belongs to 13 commercial families, and a mediacracy comprises politicians who have direct links with the communications industry due to deregulation and privatization.[28]

State intervention is less in the US media; however, market concentration near monopoly is a worse concern – hyper-commercialization in the United States controls algorithms to hoard advertising revenues and polarize messages dominated by the closed power of the stock market traded companies.[29] In France, Spain, and the United Kingdom, few of their media ownership are deregulation despite the free situation. Some are private ownership linked to the hidden power of industrial and political interests, others are family ownership without less transparency.[30]

As we have learned "knowledge is power" and the connection between recognition and economic power in the previous sections, education is essential to the power of being in all domains of participation and attainment. Taking stock of a whole situation of education for the power of being will magnify education in relation to other issues of modernization seeing that the levels, the forms, and the spaces of education can be unequal from the lens of the "power cube." Regarding this, the ways of measuring education are a series of aspects illustrating percentage, age, gender, demography, wealth, as well as location. For my Chinese peers, the investment of education in the new generation from the older generations is a hope rooted in paternalism. Parents in paternalistic Chinese modernity attach great importance to "knowledge is power" for a child by birth, scrambling for everything best to avoid losing the power of being at the starting line. The Global Education Monitoring Report 2020 notes that the power of education resources and opportunities are distributed unequally: in low- and middle-income societies, adolescents from the rich 20 percent households are three times more likely than those from the poor to finish lower secondary school. In high-income societies in Northern America and Europe, every 100 of the rich youth complete secondary school compared with only 18 of the poor youth. Less than 60 percent of countries have a definition of inclusive education to cover marginalized groups.[31] At the root of this unequal education participation, power relations linger over "knowledge is power."

The power of being concerns being modern dignity and safety whatever power relationships represent. The spaces of power have recently been a "two-way" communication making closed spaces transparent for unequal power relationships, which has to do with invited spaces – the spaces where all stakeholders come together for public dialogue.[32] The willingness to invited spaces may be working with the function of other levels, forms, and spaces of power. These invited spaces actually happen in every workplace within organizations from local communities to national conferences and global forums.[33] Making a commitment to equal power in invited spaces can be a tall order considering that power relations consist of complicated levels and forms of power, as well as incremental divided human demands for modern dignity and safety.

In conversation about power, people may interpret power as abstract from micro everyday realities. To move away from the binary understanding of the power of being, start with linking to your personal experiences. When have you felt powerful or powerless? What kinds of spaces do you enter? What forms of power do you lack? What kinds of levels are you at? How do you participate in your decisions that affect your life?

The identities that modernization accommodates are definitely not apart from power relations. In observing beyond identities, the micro-dynamics of the power of being within the spaces alongside the subtle forms of power will be an answer to powerholders who win or lose. In the face of daunting modern challenges, the remedies do not solely bank on power at one level, in one form, and in one space; rather, the remedies are determined by power relations based on the lens of the "power cube." Those who create the spaces of power are absolutely to have a larger share of power within it. In one way or another, the power of being may need an equilibrium which goes along with the approaches to modern challenging issues, whether for climate change, inequalities, sustainability, economic growth, or identity-based social movements. This is contingent on the finale of Beyond Identities – where is modernization going?

Notes

1 Castells, Manuel. *The Power of Identity Volume II.* 2nd, with a new preface ed., Wiley-Blackwell, 2010, p. 425.

2 Castells, Manuel. "From Cities to Networks: Power Rules." *Journal of Classical Sociology*, vol. 21, no. 3–4, 2021, p. 260.

3 Smith, Adam. *Adam Smith: The Theory of Moral Sentiments*, edited by Knud Haakonssen, Cambridge University Press, 2002. *Cambridge Texts in the History of Philosophy*, pp. 61–62.

4 I borrowed my view from John Locke's work, so I reckon that the power of being attached to power relationships is based on experience, and identities are nurtured at the same time. On the further note, power relationships are altered with experiences anchored by identities.

Locke, John and P. H. Nidditch. *An Essay Concerning Human Understanding.* Clarendon Press, 1975.

5 Gordon, Colin. "Michael Foucault: Selected Interviews and Other Writings, 1972–1977." *Brighton: Harvester*, 1980, p. 56.

6 "How Does the Economy Impact Gen-Z's Decision to Have Children?" *CashLady*, www.cashlady.com/gen-z-children-economy. Accessed 17 Jan. 2024.

7 "你生吗？《35岁以下生育意愿调查报告》." 微信公众平台, 我要 WhatYouNeed, 18 May 2022, mp.weixin.qq.com/s/IHPk-5600_hmjzpKSfUOgw. Accessed 25 Nov. 2023.

8 Brown, Anna. "Growing Share of Childless Adults in U.S. Don't Expect to Ever Have Children." *Pew Research Center*, 19 Nov. 2021, www.pewresearch.org/short-reads/2021/11/19/growing-share-of-childless-adults-in-u-s-dont-expect-to-ever-have-children/. Accessed 25 Nov. 2023.

9 Bacon, Francis. *Meditations Sacrae and Human Philosophy.* Kessinger Pub. Co. 1996.

10 Jones, Michael. "Lifesaving Legacy." *The University of Queensland*, 2022, https://stories.uq.edu.au/contact-magazine/2022/lifesaving-legacy-hpv-vaccine/index.html. Accessed 25 Nov. 2023.

11 Jones, Michael. "Lifesaving Legacy." *The University of Queensland*, 2022, https://stories.uq.edu.au/contact-magazine/2022/lifesaving-legacy-hpv-vaccine/index.html. Accessed 25 Nov. 2023.

12 Foucault, Michel. *The History of Sexuality.* 1st Vintage Books ed., Vintage Books, 1986.

13 Staff Entrepreneur. "Steve Jobs Biography." *Entrepreneur*, 5 Apr. 2023, www.entrepreneur.com/growing-a-business/who-was-steve-jobs-see-the-apple-founders-career-and-more/197538. Accessed 25 Nov. 2023.

14 Castells, Manuel. *Communication Power*. Oxford University Press, 2009, p. 431.

15 Fisher, Steve. "Power and Powerlessness in Appalachia: A Review Essay." *Appalachian Journal*, vol. 8, no. 2, 1981, pp. 142–49.

16 Gaventa, John and Bruno Martorano. "Inequality, Power and Participation – Revisiting the Links." *IDS Bulletin (Brighton. 1984)*, vol. 47, no. 5, 2016, pp. 11–30, doi:10.19088/1968-2016.164.

17 *Goal 10 | Department of Economic and Social Affairs United Nations*. Available at: https://sdgs.un.org/goals/goal10. Accessed 4 Dec. 2023.

18 Gaventa, John and Bruno Martorano. "Inequality, Power and Participation – Revisiting the Links." *IDS Bulletin (Brighton. 1984)*, vol. 47, no. 5, 2016, pp. 15–16, doi:10.19088/1968-2016.164.

Also see https://www.powercube.net/analyse-power/forms-of-power/how-forms-work-together/. Accessed 1 Dec. 2023.

19 World Bank. "Poverty and Shared Prosperity 2022: Correcting Course." The World Bank, 2022.

20 See https://www.powercube.net/analyse-power/forms-of-power/how-forms-work-together/. Accessed 3 Dec. 2023.
21 World Bank and the Development Research Center of the State Council, the People's Republic of China. 2022. Four Decades of Poverty Reduction in China: Drivers, Insights for the World, and the Way Ahead. Washington, DC: World Bank. doi:10.1596/978-1-4648-1877-6.
22 Li, Qiaoyi. "600m with $140 Monthly Income Worries Top." *Global Times*, 29 May 2020, www.globaltimes.cn/content/1189968.shtml. Also see Jin, Keyu. *The New China Playbook: Beyond Socialism and Capitalism.* Swift Press, 2023, p. 50. Accessed 7 Dec. 2023.
23 Harding, Luke. "What Are the Panama Papers? A Guide to History's Biggest Data Leak." *The Guardian*, Guardian News and Media, 5 Apr. 2016, www.theguardian.com/news/2016/apr/03/what-you-need-to-know-about-the-panama-papers. Accessed 11 Dec. 2023.
24 Gaventa, John and Bruno Martorano. "Inequality, Power and Participation – Revisiting the Links." *IDS bulletin (Brighton. 1984)*, vol. 47, no. 5, 2016, p. 20, doi:10.19088/1968-2016.164.
25 Unesco, and Institute of Development Studies (Brighton, England). *World Social Science Report 2016: Challenging Inequalities: Pathways to a Just World.* Unesco Publishing, 2016.
26 Couldry, Nick, et al. "Inequality and Communicative Struggles in Digital Times: A Global Report on Communication for Social Progress." 2018, pp. 6–9.
27 Syarief, Sofie. "The Media Landscape in Indonesia: The More Things Change, the More They Stay the Same." ISEAS-Yusof Ishak Institute, 2022.
28 Couldry, Nick, et al. "Inequality and Communicative Struggles in Digital Times: A Global Report on Communication for Social Progress." 2018, pp. 13–14.
29 Benson, Rodney. "How Media Ownership Matters in the US: Beyond the Concentration Debate." *Sociétés contemporaines*, vol. 113, no. 1, 2019, pp. 71–83, doi:10.3917/soco.113.0071.
30 Cagé, Julia, et al. "Who Owns the Media?: The Media Independence Project." Research Papers in Economics. https://sciencespo.hal.science/hal-03612863v1/file/media-independance-project-finalreport.pdf. Accessed 2 Jan. 2024.
31 Unesco. "Global Education Monitoring Report 2020: Inclusion and Education-All Means All." UN, 2020. https://doi.org/10.54676/JJNK6989. Accessed 2 Jan. 2024.
32 Gaventa, John and Bruno Martorano. "Inequality, Power and Participation – Revisiting the Links." *IDS Bulletin (Brighton. 1984)*, vol. 47, no. 5, 2016, p. 20, doi:10.19088/1968-2016.164.
33 Invited spaces https://www.powercube.net/analyse-power/spaces-of-power/invited-spaces/. Accessed 2 Jan. 2024.

6 Where is Modernization Going?

> *History is just beginning, if by history we understand the moment when, after millenniums of a prehistoric battle with nature, first to survive, then to conquer it, our species has reached the level of knowledge and social organization that will allow us to live in a predominantly social world.*[1]
>
> *Manuel Castells, the Rise of the Network Society, pp. 508–509*

This book began with another understanding of identities contrary to Francis Fukuyama's belief in "the end of history" and Western discourse, and it ends with the above quote by Manuel Castells. The works of these two outstanding thinkers have chiefly led me to structure my thinking of Beyond Identities in Modernity. To be frank, I do not concur with "the end of history." I did not go through the entire twentieth century. I was born in the late 1990s at a time when the Asian Financial Crisis jolted a global spillover. I am one of the new generations of Chinese who has benefited from Chinese modernization which has modernized the identities accompanying micro-globalization.

But being a member of this new generation faces more mismatched challenges and competition coupled with internal conflicting social values and external geopolitical noise. This is also true of the new generation around the world, no matter it is "modernization with Chinese characteristics" or Western modernization. I grew up in Southwest China where I shaped my more nuanced views on "modernization with Chinese characteristics." My multicultural education experience and life experience propel me to use critical thinking to observe modernization beyond identities.

The only history is the history that I sense with my lived experience. Most of us today have not been through the pristine condition of the traditional society. The traditional society was an idyllic hunter-gatherer lifestyle. What I remember is that my "traditional society" struggled with scant economic growth and lacked better education. It was a "traditional society" that Wi-Fi was a strange word. It was a "traditional society" that smartphone was in my wildest dreams. It was a "traditional society" that household appliances were manual. It was a "traditional society" that micro-globalization was far away.

DOI: 10.4324/9781003528180-7

A little over 20 years on, I am living in a hyperconnected modern world. A woman must not only have money and a room of her own but also participate in the network society if she is to write a book in the twenty-first century.

In the book *The World Until Yesterday*, the American scientist Jared Diamond reminds us that much of the traditional world persists within today's modern state societies by drawing from his own experiences in New Guinea. We have not truly arrived at postmodernity considering the Indigenous population around the world and the willingness of the human mind to be modern or return to traditional societies as we shall delve into Living in the Present – the Good and the Bad later.

Throughout the pages, I have sought to expand upon modern human lives based on research and micro realities that cut across the modernization theory and identity. I have tried to provide a fresh analysis to look at modernization beyond identities – the real intentions behind identities are to be modern dignity and safety, the power of being in modernity, and power relations drive humankind to progress in dignity and safety.

What the future holds for modernization is a big question of our time, and it dwarfs the question of a new world order led by whom. As we have seen throughout these pages, modernization paradigm must be incentivized by economic growth. To be modern dignity and safety, individuals have to weigh up different identities while searching for the power of being. The impact of the Covid-19 pandemic will be long-haul. Economies are wrestling with slowdown, inflation, unemployment, and cost-of-living pressures. The peak of modernization is yet to come under the drawbacks of modernization such as pollution, climate change, mental health, and inequalities.

This is not a book to claim another the end of history, namely, a universal modernized world or one modernization model triumphs another. Liberal democracy is an overloaded discourse. From a Communication for Development/Social Change perspective, this book looks to conclude an equilibrium befitting present and future that rises above divergences irrespective of different modernization models and identities. Identities are changeable with modernization. This equilibrium of modernization paradigm is about the participatory modernization framework in everything powered by communication technologies. Modernization paradigm linked to economic productivity and diffusion is irreplaceable. A continuing modern pathway forward will unite all modernization models achieved by the participatory modernization framework, if and when we are ready for it.

Seeking Common Ground While Reserving Differences

For the modern Chinese people, their identities are deeply bound by the power of a passport and traditions despite the opening-up to the West. For modern Westerners, their identities are identified with the power of a passport and considerably shaped by a more open society that has implications for the power of identity. Still, no modernization model will wholly displace one another as a last form of social order. Modernity is made up of the people, and the people attempt to find the power to be modern dignity and safety. Understandably, the clash of values will continue between East and West because of identity shifts with lived experience. The internal disagreements in every modernity are also here to stay. It doesn't matter whether modernity is Chinese modernization or Western modernization, as long as the brighter side is our common vision to be modern dignity, safety, and the power of being within the framework of participatory modernization.

Without the end of history, the well-known philosophy adhering to Confucianism is right for adapting to today's multicultural modernization – harmony in diversity (和而不同 he er bu tong) or seeking common ground while reserving differences (求同存异 qiu tong cun yi). This philosophy is appropriate to communication at all levels – local, national, and global. The goals outlined in Sustainable Development Goals are the pressing problems of modernization that need attention. Hence, the last goal is partnerships for the goals – "strengthen the means of implementation and revitalize the goal partnership for sustainable development."[2] To make this happen, participatory development communication will fuel the participatory modernization framework in every aspect of modern issues.

The American scholar Daniel Lerner reckoned that media participation with high literacy tended to improve more participatory modernization in all sectors of the social system although he was confident that Western modernization was superior to any other modernization model.[3] Of the world population aged 15 and older, the global literacy rate currently stands at 87 percent, up from 12 percent in 1820. However, regional inequalities do not disappear – most advanced economies have achieved as high as 99 percent literacy rate; least-developed societies have as low as some 35 percent literacy rate in Mali and Afghanistan; emerging economies have been catching up – 93 percent in Brazil, 97 percent in China, and 74 percent in India.[4]

Provided that modernization is a purposeful process, participation in this sense constantly expands the demands of humans to be modern dignity and safety. With this, we need to get rid of the myth of participation. First, participation is supposed to be a voluntary choice for humans just as free will. It is intrinsic in humankind's universal dignity to participate in any activities. Second, the meaning of participation varies across cultural and socio-political contexts to different identities. For example, passive participation in class in paternalistic Chinese modernization – students listen to what teachers say and participate in rote-learning for tests. Third, participation is a social process that reinforces other modern fields – education, economic productivity, politics, community, to name a few.

Drawing upon the inspiration from participatory development communication (see Figure 6.1), the participatory modernization framework is transdisciplinary approach to a mix of modern social changes, which is inclusive

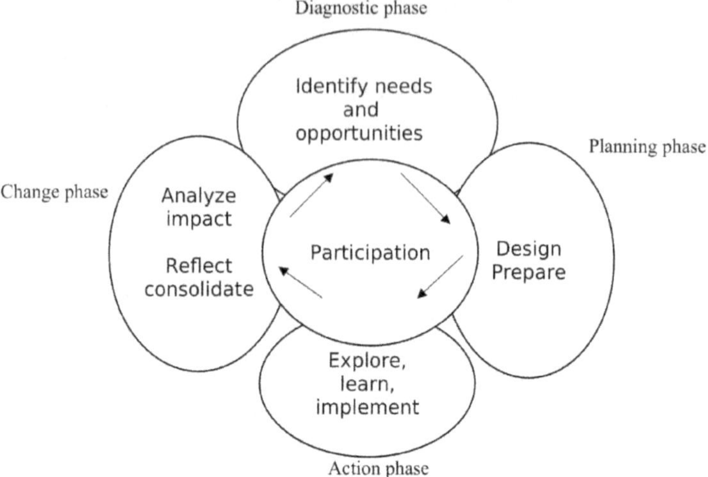

Figure 6.1 The process of participation from a Communication for Development/ Social Change perspective.

Source: Adapted from Thomas, Pradip Ninan and Elske van de Fliert. Interrogating the Theory and Practice of Communication for Social Change the Basis for a Renewal. 1st ed., Palgrave Macmillan UK: Imprint: Palgrave Macmillan, 2014, p. 124.

of economic growth of the pure modernization paradigm. Utilizing communication technologies, participatory modernization would leave room for flexibility and creativity to seek common ground while reserving differences (see Figure 6.2).

The core principle of participatory development communication is participation, but it is less a consultative, passive, and top-down approach to modernization. Participatory development communication essentially incorporates both top-down and bottom-up into substantive engagement. In a space of participatory modernization framework, all participants shall feel comfortable enough to brainstorm and negotiate.

The world today is not linear modernization. It is progressing in the network society. Depending on high mass consumption, the participatory modernization framework is to give space to express voices, negotiate and innovate modern commonalities. According to participatory video, the participatory process mobilizes people at grassroots to interact and collaborate for various issues. Participatory video contributes to meaningful engagement and offers spaces to discuss in easy, accessible ways.[5] The short-video economy has shed light on an already booming participatory modernization – a large swath of the global population is addicted to short-video content creation and sharing. Any piece of content is communicated less than two

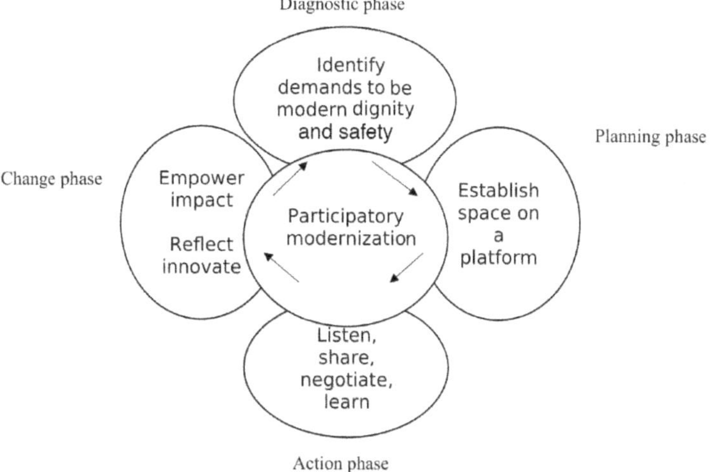

Figure 6.2 The participatory modernization framework based on participatory development communication to undertake modern social changes.

minutes long, and the content is controlled by the people instead of being choreographed. The messages are directly filmed among participants or users to strengthen communication with decision makers and communities. And the settings can take place anywhere on the street, at home, or in the car. Putting aside the regulations of political economy, TikTok exposes voluntary participation that individuals establish their participatory selves while they promote a range of interests. The total active global users on TikTok have surpassed 1 billion in 2021, and tech companies are racing to create their participant versions.[6] The monthly short-video users in Confucian China across platforms amounted to over 940 million as of 2023.[7] According to Goldman Sachs Research, the trend of short-video participatory modern economy worldwide is forecast to approach about 500 billion dollars by 2027.[8] Ten years ago, participation was very much documented in the forms of documentary filmmaking with arranged subjects.

The second decade of the twenty-first century has yielded how we communicate and participate on China's WeChat and the West's WhatsApp in the third decade of the twenty-first century and moving forward within the framework of participatory modernization. Other than the similar messaging and calling features on WhatsApp, WeChat has a bundle of participation functions featuring group chat, public account notification, digital wallet, shopping, mobile payments, games, and social post sharing. Those public accounts registered by companies, the central government, and local governments play a dissimilating role in public relations (PR) for users. A group chat on WeChat and WhatsApp is the space that can facilitate some degree of public debate in privacy. Different from WhatsApp, WeChat is a more two-way participation where people can share WeChat PR articles to their networked groups and "Moments" space.

Censorship with power takes place throughout the world, but the restrictions differ due to cultural contexts. I would employ Edward T. Hall's context theory to explain censorship – high-context cultures communicate in implicit ways and value collectivism and stability; low-context cultures communicate in explicit ways with fewer rules.[9] In communication, most Asian, South American, and Middle Eastern societies are considered high-context cultures, and low-context cultures are mainly found in North America and Western Europe. In this regard, an analysis of the UK software company Comparitech indicates that the most censored societies are joined by high-context cultures in Asia, and less censored societies are managed by low-context cultures in the West.[10] Arguably, censorship, in some senses, blocks participation. To preserve cultural norms for high-context cultures in Russia, China, India, Middle East, and Southeast Asia, censorship certainly impedes modernity from developing the equivalent participatory modernization in low-context cultures.

To visualize the participatory modernization framework, we can resort to LEGO Serious Play to facilitate participation in seeking innovative ideas for overcoming modern challenges. The Lego Serious Play methodology of participatory development communication is recognized to enhance participation process and collaboration among members of a group. It helps people tell stories of identity, past and present for building a shared future and solving problems.[11] The interplay between LEGO Serious Play and participatory development communication is that LEGO bricks inspire people to establish metaphorical narratives in connection with realistic concepts so that we are able to communicate more effectively. This levels the playing field for everyone's contribution to active and equal participation among group members. Besides, LEGO Serious Play encourages creative thinking and diverse angles when groups face challenging issues to find common ground. Here is an international work facilitated by LEGO Serious Play.

LEGO Serious Play in Participatory Development Communication: Multicultural Engagement on Energy Efficiency in Indonesia[12]

Mitigating climate change effects in Indonesia involves a number of international donors and governmental institutions. The work to improve energy efficiency deals with competing standards set by these institutions. Consultants at CAPRESE Consulting supposed that a LEGO Serious Play-facilitated workshop would be helpful for collaboration

Figure 6.3 Participants in the LEGO Serious Play Workshop on Energy Efficiency of Indonesia's Energy Future.

Source: Reprinted with permission by Friend, Eli De. "LSP-Powered Stakeholder Consultation Workshop on Energy Efficiency Policy in Indonesia." Serious Play Pro, 20 Mar. 2012, seriousplaypro.com/2012/03/14/indonesia/#more-809.

between these stakeholders and stabilization of competition. In this context, consultants designed the GIZ/PAKLIM-DANIDA/EINCOPS Stakeholder Workshop on Energy Efficiency in a room at the Méridien Jakarta Hotel on November 21, 2011. At first, the workshop introduced participants the methodology of LEGO Serious Play through hands-on exercises. Themed the future of Indonesian Energy Efficiency, participants were divided into groups to describe their common vision of the Ideal World of Energy Efficiency in 2025 through building bricks exercises. In the next session, participants were asked to share their own organization's contribution to the Ideal World of Energy Efficiency. The use of stakeholder mapping session explored the interactions and activities among the participants that have done about theme, identifying gaps and similarities in areas where synergies could tap into more effectiveness of commonality. In wrapping-up, the model building workshop promoted an agreed follow-up session held in 2012 (see Figure 6.3).

If we look at what is really happening in modernity as a whole, it is about people's perceptions. It is about how people participate in the modernity around them. It is about integrating their ideas. Within the framework of participatory modernization, seeking common ground while reserving differences through participatory development communication rebuilds power relations globally, nationally, and locally when we work together to address the downsides of modernization in relation to Sustainable Development Goals, that would be a significant transformation.

Living in the Present – The Good and the Bad

Are we living in an era of postmodernity at present? Not really. The notion "postmodernity" has been seen as a cultural and economic condition after modernity since the late twentieth century. The French philosopher Jean-François Lyotard brought "postmodernism" into philosophical discourse in *The Postmodern Condition* in 1979 with the description "an incredulity toward metanarratives."[13] In other words, a mass of people become skeptical about scientific knowledge and interpret the world dependent upon subjective personalities and experiences instead.

As we have read throughout the chapters, identity is not a permanent state for recognition. Either modernization theory or "the end of history" does not hold up when it comes to our daily dignity and safety, modernization with Chinese characteristics, migration movement, as well as power relations. The dynamism of modernization is reflected not just concerning economic growth stimulating globalization but the demands of people on the hunt for the power to be modern dignity and safety.

What makes today's modernization stand out is the network across all societies that is strengthened by communication technologies. The network society is not affiliated with any ideological dogma. It has both cultural and social importance as mentioned in Chapter 2. When the power of identity is embedded in modernization, identities echo the modern vision by and large, and separate legitimizing identities. The promise of a better life is attractive for the sake of modernization. The incredible migration movement is and will not be interrupted for people to be better than "traditional" despite in-group competition.

Diversity is not the only outcome of modernization or globalization. In the Indigenous communities across the globe, diversity naturally develops with cultural customs, regional languages, and good habits of humanity compared with city life. Features of traditional societies are with us in today's modern state societies. The traditional societies among the Indigenous people honor Indigenous identities and oppose modernization, not to mention reject communication technologies. In this case, postmodernity disintegrates into "to be better" in tradition and "to be better" as being modern.

Participation is alive in traditional societies, too. It is a fairly old version of participatory modernization at the first stage of modernization theory – traditional society. People living in traditional society of a small-scale population know each other by name and face, and they build relationships by kinship, marriage, and geographical proximity. The participation to which they belong is face-to-face discussion reaching group decisions.[14] Thanks to technology, today's participation is conducted side by side with visual mapping and diagramming, photo stories, video stories, as well as virtual meetings that save commute time and shorten distances.

Whoever has technology gains command over "knowledge is power" which reallocates resources and power to extend participatory modernization.

The slowdown of economies after the Covid-19 pandemic does not signal stagnation. Rather, economic slowdown in an era of the participatory modernization framework powered by technology is a recalibration of modernization which no longer resorts to "trickle-down economic growth" – the benefits of tax breaks and deregulation that the wealthy and corporations get will lead to more wealth for all.[15] Everyone can participate in his/her own network society to do modern economic activities via livestreaming, group discounts of online shopping, or food delivery.

It's worth noting that retailers in China initiated live commerce in 2016. The novel shopping mode enables viewers to purchase real-time products and participate in chat with a host during a live video event by leveraging social media platforms and influencers. Of all live commerce markets, China is the most mature one whose 57 percent of users have used the shopping participation format for more than three years compared with five percent to seven percent of those in Latin America, Europe, and the United States. The potential of such shopping participatory modernization continues to grow around the world.[16]

Nevertheless, the pace of modern life is not slowing down. The desire to be modernized consists in the human mind. Some people living in high mass consumption societies are nostalgic for less modern life as we saw earlier that choices in a modern liberal society will also leave people unhappy and disconnected from their fellow human beings. As such, de-modernization is bound to cultivate a hybrid form of modernization of traditionalist society in the globalized world – it is the perception of people that controls the condition to modernize, and de-modernization allows traditionalist societies to develop modernization, not need to change established value systems and lifestyles.[17]

Technology accelerates societal changes in corporate organizations, demographic shifts, rules of behaviors, and value systems. Larger digital divide emerges beyond technological scope associated with gender, age, ethnicity, income, and literacy. While Internet connectivity is on the rise, users in low-income societies struggle to close digital divide. The International Telecommunication Union's 2023 Facts and Figures report suggests that 27 percent of people in low-income societies have access to the Internet; in contrast, the figure in high-income societies is 93 percent. About 90 percent of people with access to 5G live in high-income societies, whereas 5G is in trials or mostly absent in low-income societies.[18] In Malawi, 80 percent of the total population lacks Internet access. Only 8 percent of female-led families had a mobile phone compared to 35 percent of male-led families in rural Malawi.[19] Around 65 percent of the African population misses out on the power of technology to connect.[20] What has been modernized in China, Europe, Australia, or America contradicts what is to be modernized in least-developed regions like Africa in the twenty-first century. "Postmodernity" at least does not suit the global family.

Is modernization good or bad? The pertinent question is how much modernization is best. Across the world, life expectancy has increased to 72 years on average, nearly as twice long as in the 1950s. Be that as it may, modern people then worry about how critical the aging population would be to economic activities, family functions, social structures, and caring resources. As we saw in Chapter 5, the convenience of modern life is a medley of technology and power to interact with the human body. Having said that, the declining birth rate reverses modernization – low birth rates are recorded across Asia, Europe, and America.[21]

An interesting modern trend is that the pet population worldwide is growing. Bloomberg Intelligence's Pet Economy Report finds that global pet industry is set to expand to 500 billion US dollars by 2030 with America remaining the largest pet market.[22] The falling human fertility rate has spawned more demand for companionship with pets, and people give the same care as children to pets alongside services in food, grooming, garment, training, insurance, and medical care. Though the pet market in China is also booming with a size of around 39 billion US dollars, it needs to catch up with advanced economies in terms of market regulation and better societal friendliness.[23] This pet globalization is absolutely off the track in the discourse of modernization theory. It will be mirroring the highest good and morality in people across diverse human identities.

Moreover, wars have implications for modernity economically, politically, socially, and culturally. Along with the massive loss of life, the wars in the twentieth century helped construct modernization paradigm and literature. As the world is in a moment of transformative change in technology, wars still unfold in the twenty-first century while our lives are getting better. At any period of time, the impact of wars yields historical paths of modernization calculated before peacetime.[24]

On top of that, the relationship between modernization and identity, if any, polarizes unity and division, resulting in chauvinism or racism. Analysis shows that a society will come to an equilibrium with a universal national identity, fewer conflicts, high economic output, and good institutions as modernization marches on.[25] By probing into this book throughout the chapters, we can build a fresh view that individuals' power to be modern dignity and safety has to a degree prompted modernization, and a batch of heterogeneous identities prosper with globalization. Trends around artificial intelligence (AI) will accelerate and support participation far and wide. AI is expected to replace 85 million jobs globally by 2025 and create 97 million new jobs.[26] Concerns about AI takeover go around headlines. But it is "knowledge is power" that creates AI for humans, not for identities and other species. What else?

The History of Future Generations

I was on a train from Northcote to CBD in Melbourne. A three-year-old boy was pestering his mother with harsh cries, and the mother eventually coaxed the little boy into calmness by giving her phone to him. The little boy was contented, watching a cartoon video with eyes glued on the tiny screen. This got me thinking within modernization paradigm: what is the history of future generations?

The children born between the 2010s and 2025 are called Generation Alpha. This demographic cohort is born into an era of falling fertility rates, technology-driven networks, a barrage of misinformation and disinformation, climate change, and the Covid-19 pandemic fallout. Most of Generation Alpha are the children of the Millennials and Generation Z, and more than 2.8 million births come into the hyper-modern world globally every week.[27] Obviously, this generation and future generations do not have a memory and a concept of "traditional society." Future generations take modernity for granted, seeing that they are born into an accomplished modern world where technology and information shape who they are.

As we learned in Chapter 1, the second decade of the twenty-first century was an acceleration in micro-globalization that has made a difference in identity shifts for the Chinese Generation Z like me. Sooner or later, the identities of Generation Alpha of modernity as a whole are going to be commonly formed via screens. To grasp the history of future generations, we need to look back at the history of 2010.

The year 2010 saw the release of the first iPad and the launch of Instagram. In between, iPhone 4 was unveiled as Apple's latest annual product. Competition in the smartphone market went head-to-head between Android phones and iPhone. Mobile check-in apps took off with the growth of smartphones. Facebook and Twitter had a place in the world.[28] In so doing, Generation Alpha is part of screen experiments by birth throughout their lives, and so will Generation Beta and next.

The childrearing history of Generation Alpha's parents is prologue. In keeping up with Moore's Law, future generations are more tech-savvy around smartphones and tablets, livestreaming, social media, autonomous cars, as well as AI. For this reason, they will be the enablers of mass innovation and participatory modernization. Current Generation Alpha of modernity as a whole is now seen as brand influencers and zealous consumers. Their diversity with technology shapes an unprecedented awareness of participation to name the world and pursue their dignity and safety. Mark McCrindle's Generational study reveals that Generation Alpha is set to be the most educated generation in history, and the digital surroundings will certainly influence the schooling of future generations.[29]

On the philosophy of education front, Paulo Freire has inspired a way of the framework of participatory modernization within modernization paradigm about the history of future generations. In view of the trends in digital economy, remote learning, and technological progress, education will be more of a process of liberation where students should become active participants with teachers and peers to create knowledge and change the status quo. For Paulo Freire, traditional education methods reinforced a sort of power structures to students as passive receivers of knowledge, so education should be a collaborative participation process to share knowledge and take action for the better.[30] For all that participatory modernization liberates traditional passive education, the history of future generations will not emancipate from power relations as the DNA of modernization. And their perception of power relations will be formed by participatory modernization through this "dialogical education" with tech-driven skills. As future generations are stepping into positions of leadership around the world, we can expect them to be more creative than any other previous generation in solving the downsides of modernization and changing power relations with the knowledge of participation unless they are not obsessed with authoritarian-style power retention.

Since Generation Alpha spends plenty of time on screens in education, new industries will come up by the time the future stakeholders enter the workforce. They are going to hold more jobs that highly require individual technological strengths. Growing up in a time of accelerating technology in social changes, future generations are keenly conscious that they also want to use technology to make a difference.[31]

An uncontrollable thing is reproduction assisted by technology for future generations. As noted in Chapter 2, this is an ongoing global phenomenon among Millennials and Generation Z to have babies by means of vitro fertilization, sperm banks, surrogate mothers, and genetically engineered babies. This resistance and project identity against a human's legitimizing identity for future generations will become commonplace in the long run. By estimation, over 10 million children worldwide have been born from assisted reproduction technology since the world's first in 1978. In recent years, conservative societies such as China and Japan also widely join the autonomous identity in childbirth powered by technology.[32] For future generations of modernity as a whole, they will be substantially more open and mature to the choices of fertility enabled by technology.

A safe and dignified modernity as a whole for future generations must be a space to support mental health. The current struggle with depression and emotional disorders among Generation Z worldwide is rising. According to the World Health Organization, more than 970 million people on this planet are living with a mental disorder.[33] The scale of mental illness is expanding across every modernization model. The latest insights from Harvard Medical School and the University of Queensland point out that the risk for developing a mental health disorder will massively affect half of the world's population, that means one in every two people in the world will have a mental health disorder in their lifetime.[34] For future generations with political power, they must get ready to improve the awareness and care resources of mental health through the participatory modernization framework for the people and by the people as modern dignity and safety.

Every generation is entrenched in macro geopolitical competition and micro competition in society. Future generations of modernity as a whole will not avoid the competition alongside their demands for modern dignity and safety. It could be presumed that participatory modernization has a say in modernization paradigm; then, the competition will be loaded with macro modernization models, talent acquisition, and participant versions aided by technology. In the twenty-first century ahead, it is time future generations interpret participatory modernization differently. So, history is just beginning.

What Is to Be Done?

No book can cover everything. I have striven to share a non-filtered lens to observe the micro modern world by and large beyond identities. I am from the ideologically and culturally conservative China where modernization has brought about awe-inspiring social changes for the new generation of Chinese. My proud legitimizing Chinese identity is attached to the transformative China miracle within 40 years of ups and downs. Thrifty, diligence, and peace in the Chinese values since ancient times have been the root in the Chinese blood. The opening-up to Western liberalism, my multicultural education and life experience better my thoughts to organize this book.

No modernization model is perfect, yet I believe that any modernization model creates positive social change for the people, and there are commonalities between us – dignity, safety, the power of being, as well as connections. Although this book does not talk about a cultural narrative, culture, by all means, is essential to understanding modernization and identity from Edward T. Hall's *Beyond Culture*. In this regard, participatory modernization ought to be assimilated into each modernity's cultural norms. I do not consider a macro discourse to be in the betterment of understanding modernization and identity in that bias based on agenda setting more often than not hurts people physically, verbally, and psychologically from the radicals who are enthusiastic about modern pie-in-the-sky superiority. Theory, data, research, facts, and micro realities in this book should be given thought to understanding people's modernization and identity beyond identities rather than binary and linear modern views in the textbooks and lectures.

There is an extraordinary misunderstanding between China and the West. A better understanding of people and cultures entails an understanding of their micro modernization that rises above identities. This book has conveyed such an angle that is not stuck in click-bait modern headlines. When students bid farewell to their good old days on campus, the knowledge can be out of date. There is no eternal modernization paradigm. If dignity and safety overtake identity by seeking common ground while reserving differences, if the power of being changes power relations by participating in spaces with communication technologies. Ultimately, we may be able to achieve participatory modernization and identity in any context.

For the last time, I will borrow from Manuel Castells again, "The twenty-first century will be marked by the completion of a global information superhighway, and by mobile telecommunication and computing power, thus decentralizing and diffusing the power of information, delivering the promise of multi-media, and enhancing the joy of interactive communication. Electronic communication networks will constitute the backbone of our lives."[35]

Notes

1 Castells, Manuel. *The Rise of the Network Society.* vol. 12, John Wiley & Sons, Incorporated, 2009, pp. 508–9.
2 "Goal 17: Partnerships for the Goals." *The Global Goals*, 18 Apr. 2023, www.globalgoals.org/goals/17-partnerships-for-the-goals/. Accessed 21 Jan. 2024.
3 Lerner, Daniel. "The Passing of Traditional Society: Modernizing the Middle East." Free Press, 1958.
4 Buchholz, Katharina. "This is How Much Global Literacy Has Changed over 200 Years." *World Economic Forum*, 12 Sept. 2022, www.weforum.org/agenda/2022/09/reading-writing-global-literacy-rate-changed/. Accessed 1 Mar. 2023.
5 World Health Organization. "Participatory Video for Meaningful Engagement of Older People: A Toolkit." *World Health Organization*, 2022.
6 Bursztynsky, Jessica. "TikTok Says 1 Billion People Use the App Each Month." *CNBC*, 27 Sept. 2021, www.cnbc.com/2021/09/27/tiktok-reaches-1-billion-monthly-users.html. Accessed 3 Mar. 2023.
7 "Chinese Short-Video Platforms – the New Powerful e-Commerce Weapon for Brands in China." *GMA*, 4 Aug. 2023, https://marketingtochina.com/short-videos-the-new-powerful-e-commerce-weapon-for-brands-in-china/. Accessed 3 Mar. 2023.
8 "The Creator Economy Could Approach Half-a-Trillion Dollars by 2027." *Goldman Sachs*, 19 Apr. 2023, www.goldmansachs.com/intelligence/pages/the-creator-economy-could-approach-half-a-trillion-dollars-by-2027.html. Accessed 8 Mar. 2023.
9 Hall, Edward T. *Beyond Culture*. Anchor Press/Doubleday, 1977.
10 Bischoff, Paul. "Internet Censorship 2024: A Global Map of Internet Restrictions." *Comparitech*, 16 Oct. 2023, www.comparitech.com/blog/vpn-privacy/internet-censorship-map/. Accessed 3 Mar. 2023.
11 "The Basics | What Is LEGO Serious Play." *Michael Fearne LEGO Serious Play RSS*, https://michaelfearne.com/start-here/. Accessed 02 Feb. 2024. Accessed 5 Mar. 2023.
12 Friend, Eli De. "LSP-Powered Stakeholder Consultation Workshop on Energy Efficiency Policy in Indonesia." *Serious Play Pro*, 20 Mar. 2012, https://seriousplaypro.com/2012/03/14/indonesia/#more-809. Accessed 6 Mar. 2023.
13 Lyotard, Jean-Francois. *The Postmodern Condition: A Report on Knowledge*. University of Minnesota Press, 1984.
14 Diamond, Jared. *The World until Yesterday: What Can We Learn from Traditional Societies?* Penguin, 2013.
15 Hope, David. "Tax Cuts for the Wealthy Only Benefit the Rich: LSE Research." *LSE Research*, 24 Jan. 2023, www.lse.ac.uk/research/research-for-the-world/economics/tax-cuts-for-the-wealthy-only-benefit-the-rich-debunking-trickle-down-economics. Accessed 8 Mar. 2023.
16 Becdach, Camilo, et al. "Ready for Prime Time? The State of Live Commerce." *McKinsey & Company*, 7 July 2023, www.mckinsey.com/capabilities/growth-marketing-and-sales/our-insights/ready-for-prime-time-the-state-of-live-commerce. Accessed 8 Mar. 2023.
17 Ordenov, Serhii S., and Hanna M. Kleshnia. "Demodernization as a Hybrid Form of Modernization of Traditionalist Society in the Globalized World." *Humanities & Social Sciences Reviews*, vol. 7, no. 4, 2019, pp. 1241–7.

18 "New Global Connectivity Data Shows Growth, but Divides Persist." *ITU*, 27 Nov. 2023, www.itu.int/en/mediacentre/Pages/PR-2023-11-27-facts-and-figures-measuring-digital-development.aspx. Accessed 9 Mar. 2023.

19 Heeks, Richard. *Information and Communication Technology for Development (Ict4d)*. Routledge, 2017.

20 World Bank Group. "From Connectivity to Services: Digital Transformation in Africa." *World Bank*, 10 Nov. 2023, www.worldbank.org/en/results/2023/06/26/from-connectivity-to-services-digital-transformation-in-africa. Accessed 27 Jan. 2024. Accessed 9 Mar. 2023.

21 "China Population Shrinks Again as Births Fall to Record Low." *Bloomberg.Com*, Bloomberg, 17 Jan. 2024, www.bloomberg.com/news/articles/2024-01-17/china-population-extends-historic-decline-as-covid-deaths-surged. Accessed 9 Mar. 2023. See Yamaguchi, Mari. McCurry, Justin. Cordier, Solène. PRB.

22 "Global Pet Industry to Grow to $500 Billion by 2030, Bloomberg Intelligence Report Finds." *Bloomberg*, 24 Mar. 2023, www.bloomberg.com/company/press/global-pet-industry-to-grow-to-500-billion-by-2030-bloomberg-intelligence-finds/. Accessed 9 Mar. 2023.

23 "New Trends: China's Pet Economy Is Booming." *CGTN*, 23 Apr. 2024, https://news.cgtn.com/news/2024-04-23/New-trends-China-s-pet-economy-is-booming-1t2ySp6uEmY/p.html.

24 Rostow, W. W. *The Stages of Economic Growth*. 3rd ed., Cambridge University Press, 1991, p. 14.

25 Yuki, Kazuhiro. "Modernization, Social Identity, and Ethnic Conflict." *European Economic Review*, vol. 140, 2021, p. 103919, doi:10.1016/j.euroecorev.2021.103919.

26 World Economic Forum, J. "The future of Jobs Report 2020." *Retrieved from Geneva* (2020). https://www.weforum.org/publications/the-future-of-jobs-report-2023/. Accessed 9 Mar. 2023.

27 Jha, Amrit Kumar. "Understanding Generation Alpha." OSF, 2020.

28 Gross, Doug. "The Top 10 Tech Trends of 2010." *CNN*, Cable News Network, 27 Dec. 2010, https://edition.cnn.com/2010/TECH/innovation/12/27/top.tech.trends.year/index.html.

29 McCrindle, Mark. *Generation Alpha*. Hachette UK, 2021.

30 Freire, Paulo. *Education for Critical Consciousness*. First edition ed., Zed Books, 2021.

31 Howarth, Josh. "Generation Alpha: Statistics, Data and Trends (2024)." *Exploding Topics*, 4 Dec. 2023, https://explodingtopics.com/blog/generation-alpha-stats. Accessed 12 Mar. 2023.

32 "At Least 12 Million Babies' since the First IVF Birth in 1978." *Focus on Reproduction*, 28 June 2023, www.focusonreproduction.eu/article/ESHRE-News-COP23_adamson#:~:text='We%20can%20say%20with%20a,in%20an%20interview%20with%20ESHRE. Accessed 12 Mar. 2023.

33 "Mental Disorders." *World Health Organization*, 8 June 2022, www.who.int/news-room/fact-sheets/detail/mental-disorders. Accessed 12 Mar. 2023.

34 McGrath, John J. et al. "Age of Onset and Cumulative Risk of Mental Disorders: A Cross-National Analysis of Population Surveys from 29 Countries." *The Lancet Psychiatry*, vol. 10, no. 9, 2023, pp. 668–81, doi: 10.1016/S2215-0366(23)00193-1.

35 Castells, Manuel. *End of Millennium*. 2nd ed., John Wiley & Sons Ltd, 2010, p. 389.

Epilogue

The famous novel *East Wind: West Wind* by the American writer Pearl S. Buck was a portrait of sociocultural life of the older superstitious generation of Chinese in the twentieth century China that reflected a break from tradition to modernity. It rings true today for outsiders to look into the Middle Kingdom China – the Chinese value of obedience. However, the new generation of Chinese born in the late 1990s and after 2000 is radically different from their counterparts of the West and the previous generations of Chinese. This new generation has been nurtured with domestic brands under the decentralized circumstances of "modernization with Chinese characteristics" of economic development introducing Western products owing to opening up. Readings and lectures cannot fully make sense of modernity and modernization. Twenty years ago, the Chinese beverage brands like Wahaha and Xiangpiaopiao accompanied my generation growing up and injected the Chinese economy. Twenty years later, my generation has changed with multiculturalism by embracing the West, and so has the meaning of modernization from a communication for development/social change perspective.

The role of communication for development/social change is to assist modernization and social equity by leveraging information and communication technologies. This has transformed "traditional society" in many parts of the world. The convenience of modern life spices up "to be better" all along. Today, economies are moving toward cashless society – a society where transactions are proceeded by bank cards, mobile payments, and digital currencies. In this climate, cash and coins are to become the end of history.

The stages of cashless society and methods of transaction progress unevenly. Sweden and Norway so far have evolved into the world's most cashless societies in Europe. In the wake of the COVID-19 pandemic, Asia steps up the share of digital payments. China's leading position in e-commerce has cemented its rapid adoption of digital payment via QR code scanning from megacities to rural areas. Meanwhile South Korea is the cashless champion with only 14 percent payments involving cash. For Japanese, the embrace of cashless payments is less acceptable among the aging population.[1] At times, when you have sufficient financial balance but no cash to pay in a scenario, it might be embarrassing traveling between cashless society and cash society inasmuch as the ways of payment are hugely different. In many places, cash payment is not in decline. In view of this, individuals must learn about people's micro modernization, respect each other's customs, and adapt to the multicultural world beyond identities.

With communication for development/social change, the twenty-first century bestows on us more chances to be better than "traditional" for the younger generations around the world. This means that modern people in the twenty-first century can feel free to break the traditions. In the end, it is the innate dignity that compels us to grow the power of being beyond identities.

Note

1 Cheng, Yunzhong. "Is 'Cashless' Leading to a More Inclusive Society in East Asia?" *World Economic Forum*, 14 Apr. 2021, www.weforum.org/agenda/2021/04/is-cashless-leading-to-a-more-inclusive-society-in-east-asia/.

Bibliography

"你生吗？《35岁以下生育意愿调查报告》." 微信公众平台，我要 WhatYouNeed, 18 May 2022, https://mp.weixin.qq.com/s/IHPk-5600_hmjzpKSfUOgw. Accessed 5 Mar. 2024.

"2022 Australian Flooding." *Center for Disaster Philanthropy*, 14 Sept. 2022, https://disasterphilanthropy.org/disasters/2022-australian-flooding/. Accessed 12 Aug. 2023.

"2022 Population Statement." *Australian Government Center for Population*, https://population.gov.au/publications/statements/2022-population-statement. Accessed 5 Sept. 2023.

"244m Children Won't Start the New School Year (UNESCO)." *UNESCO.Org*, 20 Apr. 2023, www.unesco.org/en/articles/244m-children-wont-start-new-school-year-unesco. Accessed 7 Oct. 2023.

"A Brief History of Globalization." *World Economic Forum*, www.weforum.org/agenda/2019/01/how-globalization-4-0-fits-into-the-history-of-globalization/. Accessed 5 July 2023.

A New Wave of Mass Migration Has Begun. The Economist, 28 May 2023, https://www.economist.com/finance-and-economics/2023/05/28/a-new-wave-of-mass-migration-has-begun. Accessed 7 Sept. 2023.

"About Migration." *International Organization for Migration*, UN Migration IOM, www.iom.int/about-migration. Accessed 16 Aug. 2023.

Akerlof, George A. and Rachel E. Kranton. "Economics and Identity." *The Quarterly Journal of Economics*, vol. 115, no. 3, 2000, pp. 715–53, doi:10.1162/003355300554881.

Akerlof, George A. and Rachel E. Kranton. *Identity Economics How Our Identities Shape Our Work, Wages, and Well-Being*. Course Book ed., Princeton University Press, 2010.

Allam, Lorena. "What Is the Indigenous Voice to Parliament, How Would It Work, and What Happens Next?" *The Guardian*, 4 Sept. 2023, https://www.theguardian.com/australia-news/2023/sep/04/what-is-the-indigenous-voice-to-parliament-australia-what-does-it-mean-explained-referendum-campaign. Accessed 4 Oct. 2023.

"At Least 12 Million Babies' since the First IVF Birth in 1978." *Focus on Reproduction*, 28 June 2023, www.focusonreproduction.eu/article/ESHRE-News-COP23_adamson#:~:text='We%20can%20say%20with%20a,in%20an%20interview%20with%20ESHRE. Accessed 3 Mar. 2024.

Australian Bureau of Statistics. "Population: Census." *ABS*, 2021, https://www.abs.gov.au/statistics/people/population/population-census/latest-release. Accessed 4 Oct. 2023.

Bacon, Francis. *Meditations Sacrae and Human Philosophy*. Kessinger Pub. Co. 1996..

Becdach, Camilo, et al. "Ready for Prime Time? The State of Live Commerce." *McKinsey & Company*, 7 July 2023, www.mckinsey.com/capabilities/growth-marketing-and-sales/our-insights/ready-for-prime-time-the-state-of-live-commerce. Accessed 7 Aug. 2023.

Bernstein, Mary. "Identity Politics." *Annual Review of Sociology*, vol. 31, 2005, pp. 47–74, http://www.jstor.org/stable/29737711.

Bhandari, Aparajita, and Sara Bimo. "Why's Everyone on TikTok now? The Algorithmized Self and the Future of Self-Making on Social Media." *Social Media+ Society*, vol. 8, no. 1, 2022, doi:10.1177/20563051221086241.

Bian, Yanjie. *Guanxi: How China Works*. Polity, 2019.

Bischoff, Paul. "Internet Censorship 2024: A Global Map of Internet Restrictions." *Comparitech*, 16 Oct. 2023, www.comparitech.com/blog/vpn-privacy/internet-censorship-map/. Accessed 5 Mar. 2023.

Brown, Anna. "Growing Share of Childless Adults in U.S. Don't Expect to Ever Have Children." *Pew Research Center*, 19 Nov. 2021, www.pewresearch.org/short-reads/2021/11/19/growing-share-of-childless-adults-in-u-s-dont-expect-to-ever-have-children/. Accessed 8 Aug. 2023.

Buchholz, Katharina. "This Is How Much Global Literacy Has Changed over 200 Years." *World Economic Forum*, 12 Sept. 2022, www.weforum.org/agenda/2022/09/reading-writing-global-literacy-rate-changed/. Accessed 12 Mar. 2024.

Bursztynsky, Jessica. "TikTok Says 1 Billion People Use the App Each Month." *CNBC*, 27 Sept. 2021, www.cnbc.com/2021/09/27/tiktok-reaches-1-billion-monthly-users.html. Accessed 25 Feb. 2024.

Cagé, Julia, et al. *Who owns the media?: The media independence project*. No. info: hdl:2441/5ej8oq8p589tbq524jeiieb7cl. Sciences Po, 2017.

Carpenter, Amanda, and Kathryn Greene. "Social Penetration Theory." *The International Encyclopedia of Interpersonal Communication*, edited by R. Charles, Roloff, Michael E., Wilson, Steve R. et al., Wiley-Blackwell, 2015, pp. 1–4.

Castelli, Francesco. "Drivers of Migration: Why Do People Move?" *Journal of Travel Medicine*, vol. 25, no. 1, 2018, doi:10.1093/jtm/tay040.

Castells, Manuel. "Globalization, Identity and the State." *Social Dynamics*, vol. 26, no. 1, 2000, pp. 5–17.

Castells, Manuel. *Communication Power*. Oxford University Press, 2009.

Castells, Manuel. *The Rise of the Network Society*. vol. 12, John Wiley & Sons, Incorporated, 2009.

Castells, Manuel. *End of Millennium*. 2nd ed., John Wiley & Sons Ltd, 2010.

Castells, Manuel. *The Power of Identity Volume II*. 2nd, with a new preface ed., Wiley-Blackwell, 2010.

Castells, Manuel. "From Cities to Networks: Power Rules." *Journal of Classical Sociology*, vol. 21, no. 3–4, 2021, pp. 260–62.

Castells, Manuel. "The Network Society Revisited." *The American Behavioral Scientist (Beverly Hills)*, vol. 67, no. 7, 2023, pp. 940–46, doi:10.1177/00027642221092803.

Castleman, Tony. "Human Recognition and Economic Development: An Introduction and Theoretical Model." 2013.

"Catchphrases Etched in History." *China's 30 Years of Reform*, China Daily, 18 Dec. 2008, www.chinadaily.com.cn/30years/2008-12/18/content_7316538.htm.

Chan, K. "Internal Migration in China: Integrating Migration with Urbanization Policies and Hukou Reform." *KNOMAD Policy Note 16*, World Bank, Washington DC. (2021).

Cheng, An, and Qiuying Wang. "*Perspectives on Teaching and Learning English Literacy in China*." Springer Netherlands, 2012, pp. 19–33.

Chen, Wei-Ting, and Ming-Huei Hsieh. "Environmental Self-Identity, Self-Efficacy, and the Emergence of Green Opinion Leaders: An Exploratory Study." *Heliyon*, vol. 9, no. 6, 2023, p. e17351, doi:10.1016/j.heliyon.2023.e17351.

Cheng, Yunzhong. "Is 'Cashless' Leading to a More Inclusive Society in East Asia?" *World Economic Forum*, 14 Apr. 2021, www.weforum.org/agenda/2021/04/is-cashless-leading-to-a-more-inclusive-society-in-east-asia/. Accessed 8 Mar. 2024.

"China: Number of Students That Study Abroad." *Statista*, 11 July 2023, www.statista.com/statistics/227240/number-of-chinese-students-that-study-abroad/. Accessed 5 May 2023.

"China's Internal Migrants." *Council on Foreign Relationships*, 14 May 2009, www.cfr.org/backgrounder/chinas-internal-migrants. Accessed 8 Aug. 2023.

"China Population Shrinks Again as Births Fall to Record Low." *Bloomberg.Com*, Bloomberg, 17 Jan. 2024, www.bloomberg.com/news/articles/2024-01-17/china-population-extends-historic-decline-as-covid-deaths-surged. Accessed 7 Nov. 2023.

"Chinese Short-Video Platforms - the New Powerful e-Commerce Weapon for Brands in China." *GMA*, 4 Aug. 2023, marketingtochina.com/short-videos-the-new-powerful-e-commerce-weapon-for-brands-in-china/. Accessed 5 Mar. 2023.

Chocron, Véronique. "Homeownership in France: A Fading Dream." *Le Monde*, Le Monde, 11 Sept. 2023, https://www.lemonde.fr/en/opinion/article/2023/09/11/homeownership-in-france-a-fading-dream_6132338_23.html. Accessed 13 Sept. 2023.

Choukhmane, Taha, et al. "The One-Child Policy and Household Saving." *Journal of the European Economic Association*, vol. 21, no. 3, 2023, pp. 987–1032, doi:10.1093/jeea/jvad001.

Collier, Paul. *Exodus: Immigration and Multiculturalism in the 21st Century*. Penguin UK, 2013.

Cordier, Solène. "'The Decline in Birth Rates Is a Widespread Trend across Europe.'" *Le Monde*, 17 Jan. 2024, www.lemonde.fr/en/international/article/2024/01/18/the-decline-in-birth-rates-is-a-widespread-trend-across-europe_6442118_4.html. Accessed 4 Feb. 2024.

Couldry, Nick, et al. "Inequality and Communicative Struggles in Digital Times: A Global Report on Communication for Social Progress.", 2018.

"Data.Ai: State of Mobile 2023: En by Localization/Final." *Infogram*, 2023, https://dataai.infogram.com/1pv12merg7e3e7axedy3mmpvvjirpge6z7x?mkt_tok=MDcxLVFFRC0yODQAAAGQfXN3KhRpyRQuUewcnuP604RFX37ROWsBPZXO9R789Ouyd_2v5FnkolcjkdpWeC6_a0d7QkKGEHuAwbxg2X51ZK2KyVQuZo07O4iOHT9s5LDUx7pt. Accessed 06 Jan. 2024.

Davidson, Donald. "Three Varieties of Knowledge." *Royal Institute of Philosophy Supplements*, vol. 30, 1991, pp. 153–166, doi:10.1017/S1358246100007748.

Davin, Delia. *Internal Migration in Contemporary China*. Palgrave Macmillan, 1999.

De Wit, Theo W. A. ""My Way": Charles Taylor on Identity and Recognition in a Secular Democracy." *Stellenbosch Theological Journal*, vol. 4, no. 1, 2018, pp. 153–78.

Devlin, Hannah. "Indigenous Australians Most Ancient Civilisation on Earth, DNA Study Confirms." *The Guardian*, 21 Sept. 2016, https://www.theguardian.com/australia-news/2016/sep/21/indigenous-australians-most-ancient-civilisation-on-earth-dna-study-confirms. Accessed 13 Aug. 2023.

Debes, Remy. "A History of Human Dignity." *Forum for Philosophy*, 5 Feb. 2018, https://blogs.lse.ac.uk/theforum/a-history-of-human-dignity/. Accessed 6 Oct. 2023.

"'Destined to Disappear': The Last Generation of China's 'Bang-Bang Army.'" *The New York Times*, 28 June 2016, https://cn.nytimes.com/culture/20160628/china-chongqing-bang-bang/dual/. Accessed 3 June, 2023.

Diamond, Jared. *The World Until Yesterday: What Can we Learn from Traditional Societies?* Penguin, 2013.

Dichter, Alex, et al. "Chinese Tourists: Dispelling the Myths." *An In-Depth Look at China's Outbound Tourist Market*, vol. 32, 2018. https://www.sedeenchina.com/wp-content/uploads/2018/12/Chinese-Outbound-Tourist-Market-Report.pdf.

"Dignity in Mental Health." *WHO.int*, 8 Oct. 2015, https://www.who.int/southeastasia/news/detail/08-10-2015-dignity-in-mental-health. Accessed 6 Oct. 2023.

Dumont, Jean-Christophe, and Thomas Liebig. "Is Migration Good for the Economy." *Migration Policy Debates*. Paris: OECD Publishing, 2014.

Dychtwald, Zak. *Young China: How the Restless Generation Will Change their Country and the World*. St. Martin's Press, 2018.

"Economic Impact of International Education in Canada - 2020 Update." *International Education Canada*, 1 Aug. 2020, www.international.gc.ca/education/assets/pdfs/economic_impact_international_education_canada_2017_2018.pdf. Accessed 4 Apr. 2023.

Eric Louw, P. "The Pax Americana and Development." *Handbook of Communication for Development and Social Change*, edited by Jan Servaes, Springer Singapore, 2020, pp. 167–92. doi:10.1007/978-981-15-2014-3_35.

Erikson, Erik. "Theory of Identity Development." *E. Erikson, Identity and the Life Cycle*. Nueva York: International Universities Press. Obtenido de http://childdev psychology.yolasite.com/resources/theory%20of%20identity%20erikson.pdf, 1959.

Fisher, Steve. "Power and Powerlessness in Appalachia: A Review Essay." *Appalachian Journal*, vol. 8, no. 2, 1981, pp. 142–49.

Foucault, Michel. *The History of Sexuality*. 1st Vintage Books ed., Vintage Books, 1986.

Freire Paulo. *Education for Critical Consciousness*. 1st ed., Zed Books, 2021.

Freire, Paulo, et al. *Pedagogy of the Oppressed*. 50th anniversary edition ed., Bloomsbury Academic, 2018.

Friedman, Thomas L. *The World Is Flat: A Brief History of the Globalised World in the Twenty-First Century*. Allen Lane, 2005.

Friedman, Thomas L. *Thank You for Being Late: An Optimist's Guide to Thriving in the Age of Accelerations (Version 2.0, with a New Afterword)*. Picador USA, 2017.

Friend, Eli De. "LSP-Powered Stakeholder Consultation Workshop on Energy Efficiency Policy in Indonesia." *Serious Play Pro*, 20 Mar. 2012, https://seriousplaypro.com/2012/03/14/indonesia/#more-809. Accessed 28 Feb. 2024.

Fukuyama, Francis. *The Great Disruption: Human Nature and the Reconstitution of Social Order*. Touchstone, 2000.

Fukuyama, Francis. *Our Posthuman Future: Consequences of the Biotechnology Revolution*. Profile Books, 2002.

Fukuyama, Francis. *The End of History and the Last Man*. 1st Free Press trade pbk. ed., Free Press, 2006.

Fukuyama, Francis. "Westernization Vs. Modernization." *New Perspectives Quarterly*, vol. 26, no. 2, 2009, pp. 84–89, doi:10.1111/j.1540-5842.2009.01080.x.

Fukuyama, Francis. *Identity: Contemporary Identity Politics and the Struggle for Recognition.* Profile books, 2018.

Fukuyama, Francis. "Why National Identity Matters." *Journal of Democracy*, vol. 29, no. 4, 2018, pp. 5–15, doi:10.1353/jod.2018.0058.

Furedi, Frank. "The Hidden History of Identity Politics." *Spiked The Hidden History of Identity Politics Comments*, Spiked, 13 Oct. 2021, www.spiked-online.com/2017/12/01/the-hidden-history-of-identity-politics/.

Gaventa, John, and Bruno Martorano. "Inequality, Power and Participation – Revisiting the Links." *IDS bulletin (Brighton. 1984)*, vol. 47, no. 5, 2016, pp. 11–30, doi:10.19088/1968-2016.164.

Gaventa, Jonathan, J. Pettit, and L. Cornish. "Power pack, understanding power for social change." *Institute for Developmental Studies, Sussex, UK*, 2011.

"Germany's Population Has Not Grown in 2020 for the First Time since 2011." *Statistisches Bundesamt*, 21 June 2021, https://www.destatis.de/DE/Presse/Pressemitteilungen/2021/06/PD21_287_12411.html. Accessed 12 Aug. 2023.

Gheasi, Masood, and Peter Nijkamp. "A Brief Overview of International Migration Motives and Impacts, with Specific Reference to FDI." *Economies*, vol. 5, no. 3, 2017, p. 31, doi:10.3390/economies5030031.

Gilder, George F. *Knowledge and Power the Information Theory of Capitalism and How It Is Revolutionizing Our World.* Regnery Publishing, 2013.

"Global Pet Industry To Grow To $500 Billion By 2030, Bloomberg Intelligence Report Finds." *Bloomberg*, 24 Mar. 2023, www.bloomberg.com/company/press/global-pet-industry-to-grow-to-500-billion-by-2030-bloomberg-intelligence-finds/. Accessed 12 Mar. 2024.

Goal 10 | Department of Economic and Social Affairs United Nations. Available at: https://sdgs.un.org/goals/goal10. Accessed 04 Dec. 2023.

"Goal 17: Partnerships for the Goals." *The Global Goals*, 18 Apr. 2023, www.globalgoals.org/goals/17-partnerships-for-the-goals/. Accessed 21 Jan. 2024.

Gordon, Colin. "Michael Foucault: Selected Interviews and Other Writings, 1972–1977." *Brighton: Harvester*, 1980.

Granovetter, Mark S. "The strength of weak ties." *American Journal of Sociology*, 78, no. 6, 1973, pp. 1360–1380.

Grant, Stan. "Stan Grant - Australia is a Country Best Seen from Above." *British Council*, https://www.britishcouncil.org.au/crossing-points/stan-grant-australia-country-best-seen-above. Accessed 12 Sept. 2023.

Gross, Doug. "The Top 10 Tech Trends of 2010." *CNN*, Cable News Network, 27 Dec. 2010, https://edition.cnn.com/2010/TECH/innovation/12/27/top.tech.trends.year/index.html. Accessed 25 Feb. 2024.

Habermas, Jürgen, and Seyla Ben-Habib. "Modernity versus Postmodernity." *New German Critique*, vol. 22,1981, pp. 3–14.

Hall, Edward T. *Beyond Culture*. Anchor Press/Doubleday, 1977.

Harding, Luke. "What Are the Panama Papers? A Guide to History's Biggest Data Leak." *The Guardian*, Guardian News and Media, 5 Apr. 2016, www.theguardian.com/news/2016/apr/03/what-you-need-to-know-about-the-panama-papers. Accessed 11 Dec. 2023.

Health, Safety and Dignity of Sanitation Workers. World Bank, 2019. *Water and Sanitation Program.*

Heeks, Richard. *Information and Communication Technology for Development (Ict4d).* Routledge, 2017.

"Heatwaves Set More Records across Europe, Asia and US." *Weather News | Al Jazeera*, Al Jazeera, 19 July 2023, www.aljazeera.com/news/2023/7/19/heatwaves-set-more-records-across-europe-asia-and-usa. Accessed 18 Aug. 2023.

Hilber, Christian. "How Can We Make Homes More Affordable?" *British Politics and Policy at LSE*, 24 May 2023, https://blogs.lse.ac.uk/politicsandpolicy/how-can-we-make-homes-more-affordable/. Accessed 13 Sep. 2023.

Hinthorne, Lauren Leigh, and Katy Schneider. "Playing with Purpose: Using Serious Play to Enhance Participatory Development Communication in Research." *International Journal of Communication*, vol. 6, no. 1, 2012, pp. 2801–24.

Hobbes, Thomas. "Chapter X: Of Power, Worth, Dignity, Honour and Worthiness." *Ryerson University*, 15 Feb. 2022, https://pressbooks.library.torontomu.ca/leviathan/chapter/chapter-x-of-power-worth-dignity-honour-and-worthiness/.

Hope, David. "Tax Cuts for the Wealthy Only Benefit the Rich: LSE Research." *LSE Research*, 24 Jan. 2023, www.lse.ac.uk/research/research-for-the-world/economics/tax-cuts-for-the-wealthy-only-benefit-the-rich-debunking-trickle-down-economics. Accessed 16 Mar. 2024.

"How Does the Economy Impact Gen-Z's Decision to Have Children?" *CashLady*, www.cashlady.com/gen-z-children-economy. Accessed 17 Jan. 2024.

"How Media Ownership Matters in the US: Beyond the Concentration Debate." *Sociétés contemporaines*, vol. 113, no. 1, 2019, pp. 71–83, doi:10.3917/soco.113.0071.

Howarth, Josh. "Generation Alpha: Statistics, Data and Trends (2024)." *Exploding Topics*, 4 Dec. 2023, explodingtopics.com/blog/generation-alpha-stats. Accessed 25 Mar. 2024.

Huang, Y., et al. "Introduction to Si: Homeownership and Housing Divide in China." *Cities*, vol. 108, 2021, p. 102967, doi:10.1016/j.cities.2020.102967.

"International Migrant Stock | Population Division." *United Nations*, www.un.org/development/desa/pd/content/international-migrant-stock. Accessed 2 Sept. 2023.

Jha, Amrit Kumar. "Understanding generation alpha.", 2020.

Jin, Keyu. "An Interview with Keyu Jin." *Project Syndicate*, 23 May 2023, https://www.project-syndicate.org/onpoint/an-interview-with-keyu-jin-new-china-playbook-chinese-tech-innovation-2023-05. Accessed 16 Sept. 2023.

Jin, Keyu. *The New China Playbook: Beyond Socialism and Capitalism*. Swift Press, 2023.

Jin, Ruining, and Xiao Wang. ""Somewhere I Belong?" A Study on Transnational Identity Shifts Caused by "Double Stigmatization" among Chinese International Student Returnees During Covid-19 through the Lens of Mindsponge Mechanism." *Frontiers in Psychology*, vol. 13, 2022, pp. 1018843–43, doi:10.3389/fpsyg.2022.1018843.

Jones, Michael. "Lifesaving Legacy." *The University of Queensland*, 2022, https://stories.uq.edu.au/contact-magazine/2022/lifesaving-legacy-hpv-vaccine/index.html. Accessed 25 Nov. 2023.

Kalb, Don. "Identity Politics, Globalization and the National State." *European Societies*, vol. 1, no. 2, 1999, pp. 269–87, doi:10.1080/14616696.1999.10749934.

Kant, Immanuel, and Jerome B. Schneewind. *Groundwork for the Metaphysics of Morals*. Yale University Press, 2002.

Katzarska-Miller, Iva, and Stephen Reysen. *Globalized Identities*. Springer International Publishing AG, 2022.

Kramer, Stephanie. "U.S. Has World's Highest Rate of Children Living in Single-Parent Households." *Pew Research Center*, 12 Dec. 2019, www.pewresearch.org/

short-reads/2019/12/12/u-s-children-more-likely-than-children-in-other-countries-to-live-with-just-one-parent/. Accessed 23 Aug. 2023.

Krausse, Reuss-Markus. *Guanxi as a Model of Social Integration.* 2010.

Lal, Deepak. "Does Modernization Require Westernization?" *The Independent Review (Oakland, Calif.)*, vol. 5, no. 1, 2000, pp. 5–24.

Lerner, Daniel. "The Passing of Traditional Society: Modernizing the Middle East." 1958.

Li, Chunling. "Children of the Reform and Opening-Up: China's New Generation and New Era of Development." *The Journal of Chinese Sociology*, vol. 7, no. 1, 2020, p. 18, doi:10.1186/s40711-020-00130-x.

Li, Yaming. "The Confucian Concept of Human Dignity and Its Implications for Bioethics." *Developing World Bioethics*, vol. 22, no. 1, 2022, pp. 23–33, doi:10.1111/dewb.12312.

Li, Zhenyu. "English Education in China: An Evolutionary Perspective." *People's Daily Online*, 27 Apr. 2020, https://en.people.cn/n3/2020/0427/c90000-9684652.html. Accessed 24 Oct. 2023.

Lipset, Seymour Martin. "Some Social Requisites of Democracy: Economic Development and Political Legitimacy." *The American Political Science Review*, vol. 53, no. 1, 1959, pp. 69–105, doi:10.2307/1951731.

Locke, John, and P. H. Nidditch. *An Essay Concerning Human Understanding*. Clarendon Press, 1975.

Lyotard, Jean-Francois. *The Postmodern Condition: A Report on Knowledge*. University of Minnesota Press, 1984.

"Main Data of the Seventh National Population Census." *National Bureau of Statistics of China*, 11 May 2021, www.stats.gov.cn/english/PressRelease/202105/t20210510_1817185.html. Accessed 09 Jan. 2024.

Malpas, Jeff, and Norelle Lickiss. *Perspectives on Human Dignity: A Conversation*. Springer, 2007.

Marx, Karl. *The Poverty of Philosophy*. Prometheus Books, 1995.

Masson, Torsten, and Immo Fritsche. "Adherence to Climate Change-Related Ingroup Norms: Do Dimensions of Group Identification Matter?" *European Journal of Social Psychology*, vol. 44, no. 5, 2014, pp. 455–65, doi:10.1002/ejsp.2036.

Max Roser, et al. "What Is Moore's Law?" *Our World in Data*, 28 Mar. 2023, https://ourworldindata.org/moores-law. 16 Jan, 2024.

McCrindle, Mark. *Generation Alpha*. Hachette UK, 2021.

McCurry, Justin. "South Korea's Birthrate Sinks to Fresh Record Low as Population Crisis Deepens." *The Guardian*, 22 Feb. 2023, www.theguardian.com/world/2023/feb/22/south-koreas-birthrate-sinks-to-fresh-record-low-as-population-crisis-deepens. Accessed 2 Mar. 2024.

McGrath, John J., et al. "Age of Onset and Cumulative Risk of Mental Disorders: A Cross-National Analysis of Population Surveys from 29 Countries." *The Lancet Psychiatry*, vol. 10, no. 9, 2023, pp. 668–81, doi:10.1016/S2215-0366(23)00193-1.

Melkote, Srinivas R., and H. Leslie Steeves. *Communication for Development: Theory and Practice for Empowerment and Social Justice*. 3rd ed., SAGE, 2015.

Mensh, Elaine, and Harry Mensh. *Black, White, and Huckleberry Finn: Re-Imagining the American Dream*. 1st ed., University of Alabama Press, 2013.

"Mental Disorders." *World Health Organization*, 8 June 2022, www.who.int/news-room/fact-sheets/detail/mental-disorders. Accessed 25 Sept. 2025.

Migration, IOM UN. "World Migration Report 2022." 2022. https://worldmigrationreport.iom.int/wmr-2022-interactive/.

"Migration Program Planning Levels." *Immigration and Citizenship Website*, https://immi.homeaffairs.gov.au/what-we-do/migration-program-planning-levels. Accessed 7 Sept. 2023.

Monnet, Catherine. *Recognition the Key to Identity*. iUniverse, 2015.

Moreton-Robinson, Aileen. "'Our Story is in the Land': Why the Indigenous Sense of Belonging Unsettles White Australia." *ABC Religion & Ethics*, 9 Nov. 2020, https://www.abc.net.au/religion/our-story-is-in-the-land-indigenous-sense-of-belonging/11159992. Accessed 17 Sept. 2023.

"Multicultural Framework Review." *Department of Home Affairs*, 14 Oct. 2023, www.homeaffairs.gov.au/about-us/our-portfolios/multicultural-framework-review/about-the-multicultural-framework-review. Accessed 10 Jan. 2024.

Natarajan, Anusha, et al. "Key Facts about Recent Trends in Global Migration | Pew Research Center." *Pew Research Center*, https://www.pewresearch.org/short-reads/2022/12/16/key-facts-about-recent-trends-in-global-migration/, 16 Dec. 2022.

"New Global Connectivity Data Shows Growth, but Divides Persist." *ITU*, 27 Nov. 2023, www.itu.int/en/mediacentre/Pages/PR-2023-11-27-facts-and-figures-measuring-digital-development.aspx. Accessed 13 Mar. 2024.

"New Study Reveals an Alarming Amount of Aussies are Skipping Meals to Make Ends Meet." *News.com.au*, 24 Sept. 2023, https://www.news.com.au/finance/money/costs/new-study-reveals-an-alarming-amount-of-aussies-are-skipping-meals-to-make-ends-meet/news-story/4debf1722c791ae7695ef7800d287dfd. Accessed 20 Oct. 2023.

"New Trends: China's Pet Economy Is Booming." *CGTN*, 23 Apr. 2024, https://news.cgtn.com/news/2024-04-23/New-trends-China-s-pet-economy-is-booming-1t2ySp6uEmY/p.html. Accessed 15 Mar. 2024.

Nolan, Jane, and Chris Rowley. "Whither Guanxi and Social Networks in China? A Review of Theory and Practice." *Asia Pacific Business Review*, vol. 26, no. 2, 2020, pp. 113–23, doi:10.1080/13602381.2020.1737391.

OECD. *The Development Impact of Migration in Origin Countries*. 2016.

OECD. Household savings (indicator). 2023. doi:10.1787/cfc6f499-en. Accessed 26 Aug. 2023.

"One Year on from the 2022 QLD and NSW Floods: National Emergency Management Agency." *2022 QLD and NSW Floods | National Emergency Management Agency*, 24 Feb. 2023, https://nema.gov.au/2022-QLD-and-NSW-floods. Accessed 12 Aug. 2023.

Ordenov, Serhii S., and Hanna M. Kleshnia. "Demodernization as a Hybrid form of Modernization of Traditionalist Society in the Globalized World." *Humanities & Social Sciences Reviews*, vol. 7, no. 4, 2019, pp. 1241–47.

"Overseas Chinese Students Spend $56 Billion Annually." *Caixin Global*, www.caixinglobal.com/2017-07-21/overseas-chinese-students-spend-56-billion-annually-101120226.html#:~:text=The%20swelling%20ranks%20of%20Chinese,according%20to%20the%20largest%20player. Accessed 15 Apr. 2023.

Palmer, Lew R. "History of the Safety Movement." *The Annals of the American Academy of Political and Social Science*, vol. 123, no. 1, 1926, pp. 9–19.

Pylypa, Jen. "Power and Bodily Practice: Applying the Work of Foucault to an Anthropology of the Body." 1998.

Qi, Grace Yue. "The Importance of English in Primary School Education in China: Perceptions of Students." *Multilingual Education*, vol. 6, no. 1, 2016, pp. 1–18, doi:10.1186/s13616-016-0026-0.

Rajkumar, Karthik, et al. "A Causal Test of the Strength of Weak Ties." *Science*, vol. 377, no. 6612, 2022, pp. 1304–10.

Ricoeur, Paul, and David Pellauer. *The Course of Recognition*. Harvard University Press, 2005, doi:10.2307/j.ctv1dv0tv0. Accessed 16 Apr. 2024.

Rostow, W. W. *The Stages of Economic Growth*. 3rd ed., Cambridge University Press, 1991.

Rousseau, Jean-Jacques, et al. *The Social Contract, and Discourses*. J.M. Dent Charles. E. Tuttle, 1994.

Saad, Ghada E., et al. "Paving the Way to Understanding Female-Headed Households: Variation in Household Composition Across 103 Low-and Middle-Income Countries." *Journal of Global Health*, vol. 12, 2022, p. 5.

Seary, Kate. "Global Identity: The Mindset for Climate Success." *UNICEF Office of Global Insight & Policy*, 6 Dec. 2023, www.unicef.org/globalinsight/stories/global-identity-mindset-climate-success.

Sheehan, Amy, et al. "420 Bushfires in Days Exhaust Firefighters and 'worst Fire Season in 70 Years' Is Just Beginning." *ABC News*, 27 Oct. 2023, www.abc.net.au/news/2023-10-28/qld-bushfire-season-worst-in-70-years/103032562. Accessed 26 Dec. 2023.

Shilliam, Robbie. "Modernity and Modernization." Oxford Research Encyclopedia of International Studies, 2010.

Smith, Adam. *Adam Smith: The Theory of Moral Sentiments*, edited by Knud Haakonssen, Cambridge University Press, 2002. *Cambridge Texts in the History of Philosophy*.

"South Korea Plastic Surgery Market Report and Forecast 2023–2028." *South Korea Plastic Surgery Market Size, Share, Analysis 2023–2028*, www.expertmarketresearch.com/reports/south-korea-plastic-surgery-market. Accessed 24 Sept. 2023.

Stacey, Viggo. "UK-China Ed Relationships "Strong As Ever"." *The Pie News*, 2 Dec. 2022, thepienews.com/news/uk-china-education-relationshipship-strong-as-ever/. Accessed 15 Apr. 2023.

Statistical Communiqué on Labor and Social Security Development in 2008, National Bureau of Statistics of China, 22 May 2009, www.stats.gov.cn/english/NewsEvents/200905/t20090522_26166.html.

Statistics Canada. "The COVID-19 Pandemic Disrupted the Economic Integration of Many Immigrants." *Statcan.Gc.Ca*, 5 Dec. 2022, https://www150.statcan.gc.ca/n1/daily-quotidien/221205/dq221205b-eng.htm. Accessed 13 Aug. 2023.

Staff Entrepreneur. "Steve Jobs Biography." *Entrepreneur*, 5 Apr. 2023, www.entrepreneur.com/growing-a-business/who-was-steve-jobs-see-the-apple-founders-career-and-more/197538. Accessed 13 Feb. 2024.

Sun, Jiaming. "Micro Globalization: Methodological Consideration." *International Journal of Arts, Humanities & Social Science*, vol. 2, no. 9, 2021, pp. 27–37. https://ijahss.net/assets/files/1631390986.pdf.

Sundararajan, Louise. "Strong-Ties and Weak-Ties Rationalities: Toward an Expanded Network Theory." *Review of General Psychology*, vol. 24, no. 2, 2020, pp. 134–43, doi:10.1177/1089268020916438.

Syarief, Sofie. *The Media Landscape in Indonesia: The More Things Change, the More They Stay the Same*. ISEAS-Yusof Ishak Institute, 2022.

Tao, Yu. "Chinese Students Abroad in the Time of Pandemic an Australian View." *Crisis*, edited by Jane Golley et al., ANU Press, 2021, pp. 290–304, http://www.jstor.org/stable/j.ctv1m9x316.30.

Taormina, Robert J., and Jennifer H. Gao. "A Research Model for Guanxi Behavior: Antecedents, Measures, and Outcomes of Chinese Social Networking." *Social Science Research*, vol. 39, no. 6, 2010, pp. 1195–212, doi:10.1016/j.ssresearch.2010.07.003.

Taylor, Charles. *Multiculturalism: Examining the Politics of Recognition*. ERIC, 1994.

Taylor, Mia. "Homeowner Data and Statistics 2023." *Bankrate*, Bankrate.com, 24 July 2023, https://www.bankrate.com/homeownership/home-ownership-statistics/.

"The 17 Goals." *Sdgs.un.org*, https://sdgs.un.org/goals. Accessed 8 Oct. 2023.

"The Creator Economy Could Approach Half-a-Trillion Dollars by 2027." *Goldman Sachs*, 19 Apr. 2023, www.goldmansachs.com/intelligence/pages/the-creator-economy-could-approach-half-a-trillion-dollars-by-2027.html. Accessed 12 Mar. 2024.

"The Basics | What Is LEGO Serious Play." *Michael Fearne LEGO Serious Play RSS*, michaelfearne.com/start-here/. Accessed 02 Feb. 2024.

Thomas, Pradip Ninan, and Elske van de Fliert. *Interrogating the Theory and Practice of Communication for Social Change the Basis for a Renewal*. 1st ed., Palgrave Macmillan UK: Imprint: Palgrave Macmillan, 2014.

Trainor, Brian. "The Origin and End of Modernity." *Journal of Applied Philosophy*, vol. 15, no. 2,1998, pp. 133–44.

Tu, Fangjing. "WeChat and Civil Society in China." *Communication and the Public*, vol. 1, no. 3, 2016, pp. 343–50, doi:10.1177/2057047316667518.

"Typhoon Doksuri: Alarming Pictures Show Floods in China, Philippines." *BBC News*, BBC, 5 Aug. 2023, www.bbc.com/news/in-pictures-66400905. Accessed 8 Aug. 2023.

"Understanding Generation Alpha." *McCrindle*, 28 Nov. 2023, mccrindle.com.au/article/topic/generation-alpha/generation-alpha-defined/. Accessed 30 Jan. 2024.

UNESCO. *Global Education Monitoring Report 2020: Inclusion and Education-All Means All*. UN, 2020.

UNESCO, and Institute of Development Studies (Brighton, England). *World Social Science Report 2016: Challenging Inequalities: Pathways to a Just World*. Paris: UNESCO Publishing, 2016.

Van Onselen, Leith. "Home Ownership Now a Pipe Dream for Ordinary Australians." *MacroBusiness*, 24 July 2023, https://www.macrobusiness.com.au/2023/07/home-ownership-now-a-pipe-dream-for-ordinary-australians/. Accessed 18 Sep. 2023.

Vesely, Stepan, et al. "Climate Change Action as a Project of Identity: Eight Meta-Analyses." *Global Environmental Change*, vol. 70, 2021, p. 102322, doi:10.1016/j.gloenvcha.2021.102322.

Wainberg, Milton L., et al. "Challenges and Opportunities in Global Mental Health: A Research-to-Practice Perspective." *Current Psychiatry Reports*, vol. 19, no. 5, 2017, pp. 28–28, doi:10.1007/s11920-017-0780-z.

Wang, Zhen-Dong, et al. "Unity of Heaven and Humanity: Mediating Role of the Relational-Interdependent Self in the Relationship between Confucian Values and Holistic Thinking." *Frontiers in Psychology*, vol. 13, 2022, pp. 958088–88, doi:10.3389/fpsyg.2022.958088.

"What Does China's Dominance Mean for the Future of US International Ed?" *ApplyBoard*, 4 May 2022, www.applyboard.com/applyinsights-article/what-does-chinas-dominance-mean-for-the-future-of-us-international-ed#:~:text=Chinese%20 students%20contributed%20%2414%20billion,of%20the%20UK%20moving%20 forward. Accessed 14 Apr. 2023.

"Why Is the U.S. Birth Rate Declining?" *PRB*, 6 May 2021, www.prb.org/resources/why-is-the-u-s-birth-rate-declining/. Accessed 18 Oct. 2023

World Bank. *Poverty and Shared Prosperity 2022: Correcting Course*. The World Bank, 2022.

World Bank and the Development Research Center of the State Council, the People's Republic of China. 2022. *Four Decades of Poverty Reduction in China: Drivers, Insights for the World, and the Way Ahead*. Washington, DC: World Bank. doi:10.1596/978-1-4648-1877-6.

World Bank Group. "Remittances Grow 5% in 2022, despite Global Headwinds." *World Bank Group*, 30 Nov. 2022, https://www.worldbank.org/en/news/press-release/2022/11/30/remittances-grow-5-percent-2022. Accessed 8 Aug. 2023.

World Bank Group. "From Connectivity to Services: Digital Transformation in Africa." *World Bank*, 10 Nov. 2023, www.worldbank.org/en/results/2023/06/26/from-connectivity-to-services-digital-transformation-in-africa. Accessed 27 Jan. 2024.

World Economic Forum, J. "The future of jobs report 2020." *Retrieved from Geneva*, 2020.

World Health Organization. *Participatory Video for Meaningful Engagement of Older People: A Toolkit*. World Health Organization, 2022.

Yamaguchi, Mari. "Japan Birth Rate Hits Record Low amid Concerns over Shrinking and Aging Population." *AP News*, 2 June 2023, https://apnews.com/article/japan-birth-rate-record-low-population-aging-ade0c8a5bb52442f4365db1597530ee4. Accessed 12 Mar. 2024.

Yuki, Kazuhiro. "Modernization, Social Identity, and Ethnic Conflict." *European Economic Review*, vol. 140, 2021, p. 103919, doi:10.1016/j.euroecorev.2021.103919.

Zhao, Liqiu, et al. "New Trends in Internal Migration in China: Profiles of the New-Generation Migrants." *China & World Economy*, vol. 26, no. 1, 2018, pp. 18–41, doi:10.1111/cwe.12227.

Index

Pages in *italics* represent figures and **bold** indicates tables in the text.

For Product Safety Concerns and Information please contact our EU representative GPSR@taylorandfrancis.com
Taylor & Francis Verlag GmbH, Kaufingerstraße 24, 80331 München, Germany

www.ingramcontent.com/pod-product-compliance
Lightning Source LLC
LaVergne TN
LVHW010935110826
845149LV00013B/2607

* 9 7 8 1 0 3 2 8 6 5 8 1 2 *